Contents

Homeschooling Essentials

A Journey of Self-Discovery, Exploration, and Preparation

Jane Thome

Journey Together LTD

Introduction

Welcome to the world of homeschooling!

Stepping into homeschooling often feels akin to standing on the edge of an expansive, mysterious forest. The path isn't always clear, and the journey can be both exhilarating and intimidating. Just as explorers of old gazed upon uncharted territories, parents exploring homeschooling face the unknown. If you've ever felt overwhelmed by thoughts like, "Am I equipped to teach my child?", "Will they miss out on socializing?", or "How will they fare in the real world?", you're not alone.

These are questions almost every parent ponders when considering homeschooling. Throughout history, many great minds were homeschooled, from George Washington to Thomas Edison. Their contributions to society remind us that education, whether in a traditional setting or at home, has the power to shape the future.

According to a 2019 National Home Education Research Institute (NHERI) report, over 2.5 million children were homeschooled in the United States. And the numbers have been steadily increasing. One might wonder why? The reasons are as diverse as the families who choose this path.

The world of traditional schooling, with its routines and set curricula, offers a blueprint. But homeschooling? It often feels like standing before a canvas waiting for that first brushstroke. This book seeks to be your palette, offering colors of knowledge, experiences, and insights.

You've taken the first step into a vast landscape of educational possibilities. Whether you're seriously considering homeschooling or just exploring this alternative option, this book will serve as your compass, helping you navigate the terrain with greater confidence.

A famous quote by John Holt, an American educator and a proponent of homeschooling, states, "Learning is not the product of teaching. Learning is the product of the activity of learners." This sentiment underlines the beauty of homeschooling. It's not just about teaching; it's about cultivating an environment where learning naturally takes place.

One of the foremost apprehensions parents have about homeschooling is the capability to teach. You may wonder, "I'm not a certified teacher; can I truly educate my child effectively?" The beauty of homeschooling is that it doesn't just lean on traditional teaching methods. Think about the first words your child spoke or the first steps they took. These monumental milestones happened without a classroom setting. Homeschooling is an extension of this natural, intuitive learning. It's about facilitating an environment of curiosity, guiding rather than dictating, and learning alongside your child.

Another concern many parents voice is the social aspect. "Won't my child miss out on making friends and interacting?" A valid point. But this is all a myth. Statistics from the same NHERI report indicate that homeschooled children participate in roughly the same amount of extracurricular activities as their traditionally schooled peers. From science clubs to sports teams, homeschooled children often find diverse avenues for interaction. There are numerous co-op groups, community activities, sports teams, and even online communities where homeschooled children interact, collaborate, and form lasting friendships.

Homeschooling is a journey with its own share of peaks and valleys. It's about understanding the rhythm of your family and tuning into each child's unique needs. We will delve into the many facets of homeschooling in this book, providing you with a balanced perspective so that you can make the choice that's right for your family.

Perhaps you're pondering, "Why homeschool?" Many reasons propel families into this journey. For some, it's the desire for a curriculum tailored to a child's pace and interests. For others, it's about strengthening family bonds. Still, for some, it's a quest for an environment free from peer pressure, where a child's self-esteem and individuality are nurtured.

As the global landscape shifts and education transforms, homeschooling stands as a testament to parental agency, offering a flexible and personalized approach. Each chapter in this book brings forth strategies, experiences, and real-life stories that illuminate the path.

Our personal journey into homeschooling began for my family after my husband, a teacher, realized something one day that inspired us to explore this path. His experience in the traditional school system had taught him that some kids excel while others struggle. Without the limits of mainstream education, he longed for an environment where he could give individualized attention and foster a love for learning.

At that time, our children were still at home, as we had resisted the trend of sending them to kindergarten, feeling a desire for something different. However, I initially had many reservations about homeschooling, envisioning a different path for our family. I had dreams of a nearby school in our little village where our children could cycle together to school, and we could experience hours of watching our children on the sports fields and other school activities while experiencing and enjoying the traditional educational system. However, my curiosity was stirred after listening to my husband's passion for homeschooling and the possibilities it could offer our family.

I was talking with a friend one day, and she helped me visualize how our homeschooling and workday life could look. She encouraged me to make time for "school-like activities" in my schedule. As a result, I started reading to our kids constantly, savoring the moments under a tree where we could immerse ourselves in captivating stories. Those reading sessions became cherished family time, filled with laughter, snuggles, and shared experiences.

Despite my best efforts to balance work and homeschooling, we soon realized that our first business venture was not aligned with our vision. The demands of the business overshadowed my ability to dedicate quality time to our children's education. There was a lot going on.

Our homeschooling journey took a turn when my husband set up a homeschooling center, and he then had time to participate in our children's education. It was during this time that we discovered the concepts of unschooling and self-directed learning. Witnessing our son's ability to teach himself, we saw the immense potential for children to guide their own learning journeys.

Life eventually led us to a foreign country, where homeschooling presented other challenges. We found ourselves in a community where we were the only children learning at home during the day. Limited resources and a transient ex-pat community tested our resilience. It became apparent that we needed the support of a homeschooling community and structure to thrive. The idea of self-directed learning also didn't fit with my need for structure, so I sought some online courses to provide guidance and progress tracking.

Returning to our home country brought a sense of stability, but we still faced the daunting task of finding our place within the homeschooling community. It took time to establish routines and discover the invaluable support and wisdom of experienced homeschoolers. As I went along, I learned to appreciate constructive criticism, knowing that it often comes from a place of love and concern.

Our homeschooling days are now mostly routine-based, offering a sense of stability and progress. Yet, we also embrace the freedom to adapt our schedule based on the weather, taking spontaneous trips to the beach or enjoying a change of scenery at a local coffee shop. Our journey includes finding balance, seeking support from homeschooling centers, and acknowledging that we don't have to do it all alone.

Through the ups and downs, I have come to enjoy my role in the homeschooling process. It has been a personal growth journey for me, learning to trust the process and be consistent. Since I know I need to fill my own cup first, I make time for my own creative outlets and reconnect with nature, which keeps me calm and patient.

This book will share more of our experiences, challenges, and triumphs with the hope of inspiring and guiding you, no matter where you are in your homeschooling journey. Whether you lean towards a more structured approach, gravitate to self-directed learning, or want a blend of both, this guide will help you shape your path.

Remember, homeschooling is not about devaluing other educational systems. It's about celebrating the myriad ways we can educate and nurture our children. Each family's journey is distinct and deeply personal, just as each child is unique.

Education activist Malala Yousafzai once said, "One child, one teacher, one book, and one pen can change the world." As you embark on this homeschooling journey, remember that your dedication can indeed change the world – starting with your child's world.

As you journey through this book, take moments to reflect. At the end of each chapter, you'll find prompts to guide your reflections. Revisit them as you progress, letting them shape your thoughts and decisions.

Like any meaningful journey, it's not just about the destination but the experience along the way. Are you ready to begin this adventure? Let's explore the enriching world of homeschooling together.

One

Your Why

Choosing to homeschool is deeply personal, and each family's reasons will be different. In this chapter, we will dig deep into your reasons for considering homeschooling. It is crucial to identify and explore your why—the driving force behind your decision to homeschool as it will serve as your guiding light and source of motivation throughout your homeschooling adventure.

Did you know that many families who homeschool find that their bond grows stronger through shared learning experiences? Now, take a moment to reflect: What are your aspirations for yourself, your family, and your children's education? Maybe your motivations go beyond the desire for closeness or educational tailoring? By understanding and articulating these reasons, you'll find clarity and strength, much like a tree drawing nutrients from its deeply-rooted foundation.

Your motivations, then, become the fertile soil for a fruitful homeschooling experience. Let's journey together, exploring the many landscapes and terrains of homeschooling together to help you unearth your personal 'why'.

Consider the following ideas as you seek to understand your "why" for homeschooling.

Protecting Your Child's Emotional Health and Safety

Many parents are driven by an innate urge to safeguard their children. This protective instinct can make alternatives to traditional schooling appealing. Homeschooling shines as a refuge amidst today's concerns about safety, bullying, peer pressure, social media, and outside influences. It goes beyond mere academic lessons; homeschooling establishes an atmosphere emphasizing emotional health, strengthening parent-child bonds, ensuring open dialogue, and providing emotional support.

Visualize homeschooling as a haven, a safe space that cocoons your children in a tapestry of unwavering love, absolute security, and understanding. Within these walls, they aren't just students; they're cherished individuals. They can truly be themselves, with every unique talent acknowledged, nurtured, and celebrated. By removing distractions and negative influences, you can give them an environment where they can thrive, grow, and blossom.

This nurturing environment offers them the freedom and the tools to passionately dive into their interests, to stand tall in their individuality, and to confidently navigate their life's course. By meticulously laying this foundation, you're architecting an educational experience that encompasses their emotional health, stimulates their intellectual curiosities, and nurtures their social and ethical evolution.

The beauty of homeschooling is its flexibility. You can tailor a curriculum mirroring your family's values, igniting their passion for knowledge. Consider the possibilities: infusing mindfulness techniques to bolster emotional stability or integrating lessons that echo your family's moral compass. Homeschooling isn't just a teaching method—it's a holistic experience, a canvas where the educational journey harmoniously balances their minds, hearts, and spirits.

Witnessing your children thrive in an environment that values their individuality, respects their boundaries, and champions their dreams is awe-inspiring.

Homeschooling isn't solely academic—it empowers them to articulate their thoughts, chase their passions, and recognize their own capabilities.

Through homeschooling, you can embark on an extraordinary adventure of molding not just their minds but their hearts and souls. It's a chance to impart lasting values, cultivate a deep-seated love for learning, and nurture resilience. Through this, you're not just shaping scholars but well-rounded, confident individuals whose self-worth knows no bounds.

Disillusionment with the School System

Ever felt a disconnect with the conventional school system? Be it during our own formative years or while witnessing the education of those close to us, we've had a few questions. Is the conventional school system, with its one-size-fits-all approach, really the essence of effective learning? These introspective moments might reveal gaps in traditional schooling, nudging you toward a more fitting, value-aligned alternative. Among these alternatives, homeschooling emerges as a beacon of hope and promise.

Reflecting on your own educational experiences, you may remember times when you didn't feel the system addressed your individual needs, interests, or learning style. Amidst the uniformity of lessons and the repetitive buzz of the school bell, did you ever feel a void? Did you ever find yourself lost in a sea of students, desiring a touch more personalization? Perhaps you witnessed your child facing similar challenges within the traditional school environment, feeling as though they were falling behind or not being stimulated intellectually enough.

There's something powerful about these moments of reflection and contemplation. They challenge pre-existing notions and introduce the concept of homeschooling – an education tailored to fit, not to restrict; to empower, not to confine.

Imagine this: A friend once recounted the story of her son, a student in a regular school setup. On one rainy day, he was once lost in thought, gazing out the classroom window, captivated by the thunder and lightning of the storm. Unfortunately, his teacher needed his attention focused on her and the work at hand. The incident prompted complaints, and the child was labeled as ADHD due to his tendency to wander off in thought. Although he wasn't disruptive, he simply wasn't "focused" in the traditional sense.

When his parents asked him about the incident, he expressed his fascination with the lightning and wondered if there was a way to harness its power to generate electricity for the grid. It turned out that he and his father had a shed where they experimented with gadgets. The teacher's concern about maintaining a structured classroom environment was understandable, but the parents recognized their son's budding interest and realized they could nurture it and provide the space for his growth.

The purpose of this story is to showcase to you how the traditional school system may inadvertently overlook children's unique passions and curiosities that children possess. With homeschooling, parents can be empowered to embrace and cultivate these interests, offering an education that is not limited by standardized curriculum or rigid schedules. It allows you to create an environment where your child's love for learning can flourish, fostering their innate curiosity and providing opportunities for them to pursue their interests and dreams.

As you embark on this homeschooling journey, remember that your child is more than a label or a score on a test. They are a unique individual with unlimited potential. Homeschooling offers the freedom to nurture their individuality and allows them to explore, question, and create at their own pace. It can be a path that celebrates the joy of learning, embraces the wonders of the world, and empowers you as a parent to be the guiding force in shaping your child's educational experience.

This homeschooling experience can be transformational for your child. Their metamorphosis in this nurturing environment can be astounding. Homeschooling can serve as the wind beneath their wings, amplifying their confidence, fueling their ambitions, and laying the foundation for a lifelong love of learning. Within this space, they aren't restricted by labels or bound by preconceived notions. They're free birds, soaring in the vast sky of knowledge. Your unwavering attention, combined with the freedom homeschooling provides, can work wonders. It can guide them toward critical thinking, cultivate an insatiable curiosity, and engender a deep love for learning.

Breaking away from the shackles of traditional education, homeschooling opens doors to a world brimming with opportunities. It's akin to crafting a masterpiece, where every brushstroke is steeped in love, dedication, and a deep understanding of your child's unique needs. Here, you don't just impart lessons; you live them. You witness firsthand the pleasures of shared discoveries, mutual growth, and the unmatched joy of dreams turning into reality.

Academic Struggles and Individualized Attention

Have you ever watched your child in their school setting and felt uneasy? Maybe you've seen fleeting moments where they appear lost, a tad overwhelmed or the opposite – not sufficiently stimulated or challenged. It's utterly heart-wrenching to witness the flame of a young mind's enthusiasm dimmed by the confines of a standard educational system. However, in the vast landscape of education, there's a glimmering beacon of hope: homeschooling. This uniquely tailored approach can be the wind that rekindles the waning embers of your child's academic journey.

Imagine a learning model where the curriculum isn't tied down by strict norms but shaped around your child's unique needs and curiosities. Homeschooling shines in its capacity to provide one-on-one focus. This model allows you to highlight their strengths and support their weaknesses, catering to their specific interests. For instance, what if your child's eyes light up at the wonders of the universe? Homeschooling might lead you both on a mesmerizing journey through astronomy, using telescopes to study the skies. If they're captivated by narratives, delve deep into literary tales from around the world, allowing them to explore diverse cultures and times. Mathematics might transform into tangible problem-solving activities, such as designing a treehouse or managing a small budget for a project. And in this digital age, a quick Google search ensures you're never short of resources.

No longer constrained by the one-size-fits-all approach of traditional education, homeschooling empowers you to create an environment that nurtures your child's strengths and supports their growth. As their dedicated guide and mentor, you provide individualized attention and personalized support every step of the way. This intimate connection allows you to better understand their unique needs, aspirations, and challenges, paving the way for a truly transformative educational experience.

A pivotal advantage of homeschooling lies in its fluidity. Lessons aren't set in stone; they're malleable, evolving to align seamlessly with your child's learning pace. Every topic, be it complex or straightforward, is broached with patience, ensuring they grasp its core with clarity. This adaptability not only embeds knowledge but fosters a profound sense of self-assurance in your child. They come to understand that the world of learning is boundless, not just limited to the four walls of a classroom.

At its core, homeschooling is about holistic growth. Beyond academics, it shapes character, fostering attributes like resilience and an enduring passion for learning. You're not just an instructor but a guide, fostering a mindset where challenges are opportunities. In this nurturing space, failures aren't defeats; they're learning experiences.

Moreover, homeschooling creates an environment where education extends beyond textbooks and worksheets. Exploring the real world, doing hands-on stuff, and connecting with others could all be part of this. Among the fun things you can do are field trips to museums, community service projects, and meetings with experts. With homeschooling, you can provide your child with a well-rounded education that goes beyond traditional boundaries.

In conclusion, homeschooling opens up a world of possibilities for your child. Every step of the way, you nurture their passions, support their growth, and celebrate their accomplishments. As you witness their transformation, you will find that homeschooling is not just about academic success; it is about empowering your child to become a lifelong learner equipped with the skills, knowledge, and confidence to navigate the complexities of the world with grace and resilience.

Academic Excellence

Homeschooling has been gaining traction and admiration in recent years. Through comprehensive research and keen observations by parents and educators alike, it's clear that homeschooling offers distinct advantages, such as consistently higher standardized test scores and unparalleled academic accomplishments. For many parents, the allure of homeschooling is rooted in the pursuit of educational excellence—a desire to see their children not just learn but thrive.

If you're contemplating homeschooling, you're weighing the transformative power it can hold for your child's education. You might believe that homeschooling surpasses traditional schooling by offering a more customized learning journey. Instead of merely adhering to a standard curriculum, you can craft a path that mirrors your child's unique passions and goals.

Consider this: homeschooling is like giving an artist a blank canvas. Whether your child has a passion for the arts, a thirst for scientific knowledge, or a desire to explore foreign languages, homeschooling provides the platform to delve deep into these areas of interest. It lets them paint their academic journey, dive deep into their interests, and cultivate a genuine enthusiasm for learning by designing a curriculum accordingly.

One of the significant advantages of homeschooling is the flexibility it offers. By tailoring the curriculum, you ensure that your child receives the individualized attention and support they need to thrive academically. Imagine the delight on your child's face as they dive into their favorite subjects, exploring them as deep as you both care to go- this is a luxury traditional schools may not be able to provide. They have the freedom to pursue their passions wholeheartedly, unlocking their full potential and honing their expertise. Your child's education can be fun and transformative, whether it is hands-on experiments, artistic projects, or immersive language lessons.

However, homeschooling is not solely focused on specific areas of interest. It also offers the opportunity for a well-rounded and comprehensive education. While the curriculum can zoom in on a child's strengths and interests, it simultaneously spans a vast array of topics, ensuring a comprehensive foundation. By intertwining diverse subjects and peppering in real-world experiences, you're not just building intellectual strength. You're nurturing their emotional intelligence and social skills and fostering a well-rounded character.

Envision homeschooling as embarking on a thrilling expedition where the true extent of your child's potential is yet to be discovered. Each day presents an opportunity to uncover hidden treasures in your child's capabilities. This dynamic and engaging journey can spark their curiosity, shaping them into lifelong learners ready to embrace a future rich in possibilities. By gifting them a tailored, individualized educational experience, you're laying down the stepping stones for them to naturally achieve academic brilliance and holistic growth.

Flexibility and Freedom

Here is another question for you. Have you ever felt confined by traditional school schedules? Yearned for more family time or perhaps a chance to travel and learn together? The rigidity of traditional education might have left you craving a more balanced experience. Homeschooling offers just that, granting you the freedom to set a schedule tailored to your family's unique needs and desires. This includes extracurriculars, travels, and special circumstances.

Instead of being restricted by set timetables, you have the flexibility to design a schedule that embraces the ebb and flow of your family's life. Whether it's adapting to different learning styles, accommodating extracurricular activities, incorporating family outings, or traveling the world, homeschooling allows you to weave learning seamlessly into your everyday experiences.

Imagine waking up in the morning to the joy of knowing that the day ahead is yours to shape. You can start the day with a family breakfast, where conversations flow freely and ideas take flight. Engaging in meaningful discussions, sharing insights, and nurturing each other's passions becomes a cherished part of your homeschooling routine. As the day unfolds, homeschooling ensures your children aren't just confined to textbooks. They can passionately delve into topics that intrigue them. Maybe it's an engrossing novel that whisks them to a different time, a hands-on experiment in the backyard that piques their scientific curiosity, or even a nature walk where every leaf and stone unravels a story. The world becomes their classroom, nurturing their inherent sense of wonder.

And with this style of education, the traditional pressures fade away. Gone are the days of hurriedly cramming assignments to meet looming deadlines. Here, time is a generous ally. They can dive deep into subjects that spark their interest, pursue their favorite hobbies, or dedicate time to hone specific skills. This freedom empowers them to truly embrace their individuality.

Beyond the flexible schedule, homeschooling cultivates a more balanced lifestyle, where stress and overwhelm take a backseat. By tailoring the schedule to accommodate your family's unique rhythms, you establish a harmonious blend of academic pursuits, quality family time, and personal growth. Homeschooling becomes a catalyst for reducing stress, fostering stronger family connections, and nurturing a sense of well-being.

Imagine, too, the joy of unplanned adventures. With homeschooling, a day at the museum can turn into a riveting history lesson. A walk in the park can become a biology class. Every journey, whether pre-planned or spontaneous, becomes a part of the curriculum, breaking the monotony and making learning dynamic and engaging.

In essence, homeschooling is not just about education; it's a lifestyle choice. It's about understanding that every moment can be a learning opportunity and that every day can be tailored to nurture both the mind and the heart. With homeschooling, you and your family can truly savor life on your own terms, fostering an environment where learning is as natural as breathing.

Family Values and Beliefs

When you decide to homeschool, you're embarking on a journey that goes beyond academics. This is your chance to create an education that fits your family's values, beliefs, and aspirations. When you homeschool your kids, you can seamlessly incorporate your cultural, religious, or philosophical perspectives into their learning experiences, nurturing their character and shaping their worldview. To put it in perspective, imagine a family deeply rooted in environmental conservation. With homeschooling, their curriculum could seamlessly sculpt lessons around sustainability, recycling, and nature conservation, making learning resonate with real-world concerns.

Homeschooling is an empowering paradigm shift. It's not just about intellectual enhancement but also about nourishing emotional, moral, and social growth. Freed from the rigidities of standardized schooling, your child's natural inquisitiveness thrives in an environment that celebrates their distinct identity.

Imagine starting each day with a moment of reflection, where you can share your family's values and beliefs with your children. Whether it's through morning prayers, discussions about important ethical principles, or teachings about cultural traditions, homeschooling creates the space for these meaningful exchanges. You can infuse their education with the teachings and practices that are dear to your family, providing a solid foundation for their moral and spiritual growth.

Incorporating family values and beliefs into homeschooling goes beyond mere theoretical lessons. It involves embodying those principles in your everyday interactions and activities. For example, if your family values compassion, you can engage in regular acts of kindness together, such as volunteering at local charities or reaching out to help neighbors in need. Through these experiences, your children not only learn about empathy but also witness firsthand the power of their actions in making a positive difference in the world.

In traditional schooling, subjects like financial literacy or community engagement might be relegated to specific grades or occasional lessons. But in homeschooling, the fluidity of the approach ensures that such vital life lessons, anchored firmly in your family's ethos, aren't merely theoretical concepts. Instead, they're brought to life, practiced, and experienced. Engaging children in family budget planning, community events, or sustainable living projects can illustrate the concept. This ensures that learning isn't confined to the pages of textbooks but finds expression in real-world applications, giving children tools they can use throughout their lives.

The flexibility of homeschooling could allow you to celebrate and embrace your family's cultural heritage. You can incorporate cultural festivals, traditional music and dance, and culinary experiences into their learning journey. An example of this may look like during a unit on world history, you dive deeper into the rich tapestry of your family's cultural background, exploring the traditions, customs, and historical significance of your ancestors. This not only enriches their understanding of the world but also fosters a deep appreciation for their own heritage.

The adaptability of homeschooling enables you to integrate your family's values and beliefs into the daily rhythm of their education. You can schedule time for reflection, prayer, or meditation, ensuring that these practices are woven into their learning journey. Moreover, you have the freedom to align their education with important religious observances, cultural celebrations, or philosophical reflections, giving them a deeper understanding of their place in the world and their connection to something greater than themselves.

In summary, homeschooling is not merely an alternative teaching method—it's a transformative journey. It celebrates the essence of what makes each family distinctive and unique. The shared beliefs, experiences, and traditions form the robust foundation upon which children's characters are molded. These guide their choices, shape their worldviews, and reinforce a sense of belonging and identity. In the embrace of homeschooling, families find a harmonious fusion of education, core values, and the profound love that ties each member together, forging bonds that last a lifetime.

Strengthening Family Connections

In today's fast-paced world, many families find themselves caught in a whirlwind of activities, responsibilities, and fragmented schedules. The modern family dynamic often sees members dispersed, with minimal overlap in their daily routines. It's within this context that homeschooling emerges as an oasis—a haven of connection and shared experiences. Much like a garden that flourishes with consistent care and attention, homeschooling provides fertile ground to nurture and strengthen family ties. So if building a strong and close-knit family unit is a priority for you, homeschooling can be a wonderful opportunity to strengthen family connections.

Consider the typical family where school and work schedules dominate. The sun rises, children hustle to catch school buses, parents dash to work, and everyone reconvenes briefly in the evening, often exhausted. Such a routine, while commonplace, often lacks the ingredients essential for deepening family connections. With homeschooling, you have shared moments of learning, and exploration become the building blocks of a strong family bond. Whether it's taking on educational adventures, engaging in creative projects, or simply having meaningful conversations during meal times, these experiences create lasting memories and forge unbreakable connections among family members.

Picture beginning each day with your children, sharing breakfast together, and engaging in meaningful conversations. This unhurried time together sets the tone for the day, fostering a sense of connection and unity. As you embark on your homeschooling journey, you can prioritize family time and create routines that allow for shared experiences and deepening relationships.

When my children were younger, they enjoyed a more relaxed morning routine. Both were up early and usually rose filled with imagination and plans, eager to delve into them. I often found one of them sitting and drawing at the table, and the rest of us sometimes joined in at her request. Meanwhile, her brother frequently disappeared to the garage, engrossed in some grand Lego project to begin his day. And even though school days weren't always perfect, there was a profound sense of peace and joy in how we started our day, which set the tone for the remainder of it. They both still prefer easing into their day.

Homeschooling offers countless opportunities for shared learning experiences that strengthen family connections. It transforms mundane weekdays into a series of adventures. Families don't just read about historical landmarks; they pack bags, visit them, and delve into stories, feeling the weight of history beneath their feet. Science isn't confined to textbooks; it's in the backyard experiments, the nature walks observing flora and fauna, and the stargazing sessions on clear nights. Every activity, every question posed, and every discovery made cements family bonds. The joy of shared learning isn't just educational—it's profoundly relational.

Moreover, homeschooling provides opportunities for siblings to build close relationships as they spend more time together throughout the day. Being together more often allows siblings to support and learn from one another. They can collaborate on projects, engage in discussions, share their knowledge and experiences, and support one another's learning journey. Siblings can become not only classmates but also lifelong friends, forming a strong support system and sharing a unique understanding of each other. These interactions foster empathy, teamwork, and a sense of camaraderie that extends beyond the homeschooling years.

Homeschooling also promotes open, meaningful communication between parents and children. In a world drowning in fleeting digital interactions, the depth of conversation homeschooling cultivates is a breath of fresh air. These aren't just cursory exchanges but profound dialogues spanning values, beliefs, challenges, aspirations, and everything in between. They become crucial touchpoints, strengthening mutual trust and understanding. Through these conversations, parents seamlessly pass down family traditions, values, and wisdom, bridging generational gaps.

In addition to academic pursuits, homeschooling provides the flexibility to engage in shared hobbies, creative projects, or physical activities as a family. Whether it's cooking together, pursuing a shared interest in art or music, or engaging in outdoor adventures, these shared activities promote teamwork, cooperation, and a sense of togetherness. These moments of shared joy and accomplishment become cherished memories that bind family members together.

Homeschooling also allows for the integration of family rituals and traditions into the daily routine. Whether it's a regular family game night, a weekly family movie night, or a special family meal to celebrate cultural holidays, these rituals create a sense of continuity, belonging, and shared identity. They provide a framework for strengthening family connections and creating a sense of unity and belonging.

In essence, homeschooling provides a unique opportunity to strengthen family connections and build a close-knit family unit. Through shared experiences, open communication, and the prioritization of family time, homeschooling fosters deeper relationships and creates lifelong memories. It is a journey that brings families closer together, nurturing bonds that withstand the test of time and creating a foundation of love, support, and togetherness.

Fostering a Sense of Exploration

In being a parent, you are acutely aware of the sense of wonder and curiosity in your children. Their potential isn't just something you observe; it's something you deeply believe in. The amazing thing about homeschooling is how it fosters and nurtures this sense of exploration, allowing your kids to discover themselves, gain knowledge, and develop their talents.

When you homeschool, your kids are empowered to embrace their curiosity as a guiding force. With each step they take, they can acquire knowledge and develop critical thinking skills, problem-solving abilities, and a genuine passion for learning. It teaches them to ask probing questions, seek answers, and challenge conventional wisdom. Developing their exploratory mindset propels them toward intellectual growth and personal development.

In the homeschooling environment, your child has the freedom to chart their own course. Imagine they're in a vast library, free to pick any book, dive into any subject, and connect seemingly unrelated topics. You can let your kids experiment fearlessly when you homeschool them. They can dive deep into their favorite subjects, explore tangents and interdisciplinary connections, and uncover hidden talents that may have otherwise remained dormant. They can engage in hands-on projects, collaborate with peers, and cultivate their creativity in ways that traditional classrooms may not always allow. As a homeschooler, you get to paint their own educational journey, blending academics with interests and creativity.

This tailor-made educational experience does more than impart knowledge—it ignites a flame. A flame that symbolizes a profound love for learning, transcending the rigid confines of standard textbooks and routine exams. Through this journey, your child doesn't just evolve into a student but a lifelong learner. They are constantly fueled by an unending quest for knowledge, a thirst for fresh ideas, and a strong belief in their innate capability to bring about meaningful change in the world.

In essence, with homeschooling, your kids can explore their interests, passions, and hobbies more deeply. It gives them the gift of time to work on meaningful projects, do in-depth research, and master skills at their own pace. It nurtures their natural curiosity, empowering them to uncover their unique talents and develop a strong sense of self.

Financial Considerations

Just as with many aspects of life, your financial situation plays a pivotal role in the homeschooling decision. Some families find that due to their specific financial circumstances, homeschooling emerges as a practical and cost-effective choice. Understanding the financial realm and available resources enables you to effectively wade through homeschooling's monetary side, aligning with your family's financial well-being.

One undeniable perk of homeschooling is its potential to be a more affordable alternative compared to private education. Consider this: private school fees can sometimes be equivalent to buying a brand-new car every year. Redirecting this substantial sum to homeschooling means you're investing in a personalized educational journey for your child. Homeschooling offers the gift of adaptability; you're at liberty to modify the syllabus, select fitting learning materials, and find budget-friendly resources.

Furthermore, homeschooling can be seen as a solution to the snowballing costs associated with traditional schooling. Think of all the regular expenses: daily commutes, distinctive uniforms, after-school activities, the ever-growing list of school supplies, and the routine lunches out. By adopting homeschooling, you can potentially eliminate these costs. Now, envision repurposing those savings into unique educational tools or an insightful field trip that brings learning to life.

When considering the financial implications of homeschooling, it is crucial to explore the wealth of resources and cost-effective curriculum options available. There are numerous online platforms, libraries, and educational organizations that offer free or low-cost resources, textbooks, and learning materials. You can even tap into virtual learning communities, connect with other homeschooling families, and share resources, creating a supportive network.

In the modern age, homeschooling also opens doors to cutting-edge educational avenues. Platforms offering online courses or virtual academies often come with adjustable pricing models and tailor-made curriculums. Imagine accessing top-tier education at a fraction of mainstream schooling costs!

With a dash of initiative and a sprinkle of resourcefulness, homeschooling becomes financially attainable. Commit to researching, contrasting curriculum choices, and scouting both free and economic resources. Drafting a comprehensive budget encompassing learning tools, excursions, and extra-curricular guarantees not just an enriching homeschooling experience but also your family's fiscal security.

Here's a thought: why not make budgeting a practical lesson for your children? Let them handle the homeschooling budget, teaching them the principles of financial planning, saving, and informed spending. Such hands-on financial lessons will not only enhance their mathematical skills but also prepare them for a future where they can confidently manage their finances.

In conclusion, let the financial facet of homeschooling inspire ingenuity and imaginative solutions, not apprehension. By meticulous planning and harnessing affordable avenues, you can homeschool in harmony with your family's ethos and financial aspirations.

Curiosity and Open-mindedness

At times, the decision to homeschool isn't just born out of necessity or discontent with traditional schooling. Instead, it's sparked by a potent mix of curiosity and the desire to explore varied educational paths. Hearing tales from friends, describing how their children thrived in the free-spirited environment of homeschooling, much like flowers blossoming in the wild. Their narratives of rich learning experiences, tailor-made education, and the tight-knit bond within their homeschooling circles might have caught your ear.

In the dynamic landscape of education, it's only human to wonder about alternatives to conventional classrooms. Perhaps the concept of homeschooling has subtly crept into your thoughts, whispering promises of unlimited opportunities, unmatched creativity, and an exclusive educational journey for your loved ones. Even without a clear challenge in the existing educational framework, there might be a part of you yearning to experience this broad horizon and dive deep into the realm of homeschooling.

This instinctive pull is a signal, highlighting your openness to the expansive world that homeschooling promises. Embrace this spirit of adventure, as this could lead you to uncharted territories full of hidden gems, newfound interests, and revolutionary educational experiences that indelibly mark your children's lives.

Think of homeschooling as a blank canvas, where you're the artist, painting an education bursting with color tailored to your family's needs. It creates an ambiance that fosters curiosity, where learning isn't restricted by traditional modules. It gives your children the liberty to chase their curiosities and gain knowledge in sync with their distinct personalities and dreams.

In the realm of homeschooling, the world becomes your classroom. You have the flexibility to venture beyond the confines of textbooks, unlocking a world of resources, experiences, and opportunities that cater to your family's specific interests and passions. Imagine learning history from age-old manuscripts, running science experiments on your dining table, soaking in nature's magnificence, or engaging in artistic creations; your boundaries are as vast as your imagination.

Through homeschooling, driven by curiosity and open-mindedness, you become the architect of your family's education. You can choose from a variety of educational philosophies and customize your approach to fit your family's values. Whether you're looking for holistic and meaningful learning, you can incorporate Montessori, Waldorf, or any of the classical approaches you would rather prefer.

And remember, within the homeschooling community, you will find a tremendous amount of fellow explorers who are passionate about education and dedicated to supporting one another on this less traveled path. Connect with like-minded individuals, join homeschooling co-ops, attend gatherings and conferences, and tap into the collective wisdom and experiences of those who have embarked on similar journeys. The support, camaraderie, and shared resources within the homeschooling community will invigorate and inspire you as you navigate this uncharted terrain.

So, if the idea of homeschooling tugs at your heartstrings, beckoning you with its promises of curiosity-driven exploration and open-mindedness, embrace this calling. Embrace the joy of uncovering new educational frontiers, witnessing your children's eyes light up with wonder and discovery, and fostering a deep love for learning within your family.

Remember, homeschooling is not just about what happens within the walls of your home; it's about embracing the world as your playground and nurturing a lifelong love for knowledge and discovery. Embrace this spirit of curiosity and open-mindedness, and let it guide you on an extraordinary educational journey that will forever shape the hearts and minds of your children. The wonders that await your family are ready to be unveiled.

Having unraveled a comprehensive spectrum of insights, the ball is now in your court. It's now your turn to introspect which of these ideas resonates deeply with you. Reflect deeply upon these insights, amalgamating them with any other personal motivations that stir your soul. Keep in mind that homeschooling is not a monolithic entity. Every family's path into homeschooling is unique, shaped by their individual circumstances, values, and dreams. By delving deep into your foundational 'why,' you embark upon the inaugural phase of sculpting a homeschooling voyage that's in perfect resonance with your family's envisioned goals and dreams.

Now, write down your thoughts and feelings below of your why. This activity is essential as it will serve as a compass, guiding you through the challenges and reaffirming your commitment during difficult times. It will serve as a source of inspiration and a reminder of your motivation when times get difficult.

What is <u>Your Why?</u>

_____

_____

_____

_____

Two

Looking to the Future

So now that you've identified your why, let's figure out where you want to go during this homeschooling adventure! Thinking about the future and the outcomes you hope to achieve for your kids as you embark on this educational journey is essential. What outcomes do you envision for your children's education? What qualifications and opportunities do you want to provide for them? Your priorities and how you structure your homeschooling will depend on these considerations. In this session, we'll delve into the significance of forward-thinking. And to cap it off, we'll offer a writing exercise to steer your reflections. Let's start this journey of learning together, and let's see where it takes us!

Defining Educational Goals: A Symphony of Vision and Values

We need to have conversations about the future because it plays a vital role in shaping our educational approach. It's important to consider what opportunities your children should have as they progress in their education. While degrees may hold societal importance, remember that the ultimate choice lies with your children. However, exploring the options and pathways that can open doors for them in the wider world is worth exploring.

When it comes to homeschooling, you possess the remarkable opportunity to shape education according to your family's values, aspirations, and priorities.

Take a moment to reflect on what truly matters to you and your children. Is it fostering a love for learning? Nurturing critical thinking skills? Building strong character? Whatever your goals may be, homeschooling empowers you to design an educational experience that resonates with your family's unique vision.

Consider the subjects and skills you want your children to explore and master. Take some time to observe your children's interests and natural strengths. Do they show particular inclinations or passions? Even if they are still young, you can start providing them with more exposure to these interests. This will allow them to explore and develop their talents further. By considering their interests and strengths, you can start creating a tailored educational experience that nurtures their potential.

Looking ahead, consider what your children need to achieve their goals. Consider the skills, knowledge, and experiences that will set them on the right path. This will provide you with a flight plan for curriculum choices, extracurricular activities, and other opportunities you want to explore. Remember, homeschooling is not just about textbooks and academic tests; it's also about the non-curricular activities that can help them grow and develop holistically. It's about providing a well-rounded education that consists of the arts, physical fitness, and practical life skills. Embrace integrated approaches, where different subjects seamlessly blend together and encourage project-based learning to ignite your child's curiosity and unlock their boundless creativity.

Broadening Horizons: Qualifications and the Kaleidoscope of Opportunities

One common concern for new homeschooling parents is the question of qualifications and opportunities. Rest assured, homeschooling offers numerous pathways for your child to obtain the qualifications they need while embracing a personalized and enriching educational journey.

Accreditation and future high school diplomas may be on your mind. While it's true that homeschoolers have alternative pathways to obtaining these credentials, it's essential to know that there are recognized options available. To find the best fit for your child's educational journey, take the time to research accredited homeschool programs and associations that offer diplomas. These programs often provide structured curricula, guidance, and support, which can be particularly helpful for parents who are new to homeschooling. Chapter 5 and Chapter 6 of this book will delve deeper into different homeschooling approaches and explore the various types and styles of homeschooling, giving you valuable insights into choosing the right path that best suits your family's needs and goals.

That being said, you will want to ensure you are keeping track of academic records and documenting achievements. By doing so, you will create a comprehensive portfolio that showcases their incredible journey of growth and learning. This portfolio can include samples of their work, projects, awards, and any other significant accomplishments. It serves as a tangible representation of their educational progress and can be a valuable asset when applying to colleges or pursuing future career opportunities.

But the range of possibilities extends far beyond traditional academic pursuits. Homeschooling is about nurturing well-rounded individuals who are prepared to embrace a world of opportunities. By taking control of your child's education, you empower them to explore their passions, develop unique skills, and discover their true potential. Here are some exciting opportunities that homeschooling can provide:

- Entrepreneurial Endeavors

Homeschooling can kindle an entrepreneurial spirit within children, fostering independence, creativity, and adaptability, making them well-suited for unique career paths and unconventional professions. Encourage your children to dream big and explore their passions. With homeschooling as their foundation, they can carve their own paths and make a meaningful impact in the world.

Whether they start a small business, create innovative products, or engage in social entrepreneurship, homeschooling provides a flexible and supportive environment for your child to develop real-world skills and cultivate their entrepreneurial mindset.

- Pursuing Unconventional Professions

With the freedom and flexibility of homeschooling, your child can explore unconventional professions that align with their passions and talents. From art and music to sustainable agriculture and technology, homeschooling offers the opportunity to delve deeper into subjects that traditional schooling might not adequately cover. Your child can develop specialized skills and expertise that set them apart in their chosen field, allowing them to pursue fulfilling and unconventional career paths.

- Personal Growth and Life Skills

Homeschooling provides a unique platform for personal growth and the development of essential life skills. In addition to academic subjects, you can prioritize teaching your child practical skills such as critical thinking, problem-solving, communication, time management, and self-motivation. These skills lay a strong foundation for their future success, enabling them to adapt to various challenges and navigate the ever-changing landscape of the modern world.

- Community Engagement and Volunteering

Another fantastic opportunity that homeschooling offers is the chance to actively engage with the local community. Your child can participate in volunteering activities, internships, and community service projects. By immersing themselves in these experiences, they gain empathy, a sense of social responsibility, and a broader perspective of the world. These interactions cultivate qualities that are highly valued by colleges and future employers.

- Embracing the Future/ Igniting Your Child's Boundless Potential

If you don't quite know yet, give yourself the time to observe and figure it out. If your kids are old enough, engage them in this process. Involve them in discussions about their future aspirations and how homeschooling can support their goals. As you guide your children on this educational adventure, encourage them to take ownership of their learning and pursue personal growth. Beyond academic pursuits, remember that homeschooling is about fostering a love for lifelong learning. Help them develop critical thinking skills, nurture their emotional intelligence, and cultivate a sense of curiosity that will accompany them throughout their lives. By including them, you empower them to take ownership of their education and foster a sense of purpose and motivation.

Remember, as a homeschooling parent, you have the freedom to tailor your child's education to their unique needs and aspirations. Embrace the kaleidoscope of opportunities that homeschooling brings, allowing your child to discover their passions, develop their talents, and make a meaningful impact in the world. The journey may be unconventional, but with your support and their dedication, the possibilities are truly endless.

To embark on this journey, start by setting academic targets that align with your aspirations. It's time for a writing exercise that will serve as a roadmap for your homeschooling journey. Take a moment to reflect and write down your thoughts on the future:

Where do you see your children heading in their education?

_____

_____

_____

_____

What aspirations and goals do you have for them? What goals do your kids have for themselves?

_____

_____

_____

_____

What qualifications or opportunities do you want to include in their educational journey?

_____

_____

_____

_____

Consider their interests and strengths. How can you nurture and support these areas of passion?

_____

_____

_____

_____

What skills and knowledge do you believe are essential for their future success?

_____

_____

_____

_____

How can you incorporate these aspirations and goals into your homeschooling curriculum and activities?

_____

_____

_____

_____

Are there any specific resources, programs, or experiences you want to explore to help them reach their potential?

_____

_____

_____

_____

By completing this writing exercise, you create a roadmap that can guide you during challenging times and provide inspiration and direction. It will serve as a reminder of the purpose behind your decision to homeschool and help you stay focused on your children's future.

As you move forward in your homeschooling journey, remember that this roadmap is not set in stone. It can evolve and adapt as your children grow, and new opportunities arise. Embrace the process of exploration and discovery, and give yourself the grace and freedom to adjust your plans accordingly. The future is full of possibilities, and homeschooling provides the flexibility to shape an educational experience that aligns with your children's dreams and aspirations. The only constant in life is change, and your child will change and evolve as you continue with this homeschooling journey.

Three

Embracing Your Giants – Dealing with Your Own & Others' Criticisms in Homeschooling

In the realm of homeschooling, you will inevitably encounter various criticisms and opinions from others. In this chapter, we will address these homeschooling criticisms, explore strategies for overcoming them and discuss how to stay focused on your own journey. Remember that the decision to homeschool is deeply personal, and it's important to trust in yourself and your ability to provide an enriching educational experience for your children. Remember why you have chosen this path rather than comparing yourself to others.

Socialization Misconceptions

One of the frequent criticisms directed at homeschooling is the concern about the social development of homeschooled children compared to their traditionally-schooled peers. It is often assumed that homeschooling isolates children from social interactions, leaving them devoid of the valuable experiences that come from interacting with a diverse range of individuals. However, this assumption is far from the truth. In fact, homeschooling families have a multitude of opportunities for socialization that extend well beyond the confines of a traditional classroom. As the homeschooling parent, you must include it in your plan, how you will give your family the necessary interactions with others.

Homeschooling families can embrace a wide variety of social interactions, fostering meaningful connections and diverse experiences for children. Extracurricular activities play a vital role in expanding their social horizons. Homeschooled children can participate in various activities such as sports teams, art classes, music lessons, dance studios, and theater groups. These engagements not only provide opportunities for skill development but also enable them to interact with peers who share similar interests and passions.

Another avenue for socialization is joining homeschooling groups or co-ops, where families come together to share resources, ideas, and experiences. These groups often organize field trips, educational outings, and group activities, allowing children to engage in collaborative learning and form lasting friendships. Within these supportive communities, children have the chance to interact with peers of different ages, fostering a sense of camaraderie and empathy that transcends traditional grade-level boundaries.

Community involvement is another essential aspect of homeschooling socialization. Families can engage with their local community through volunteering, participating in service projects, or attending community events. Places of worship often provide a nurturing environment for social connections, where homeschooling families can join youth groups or participate in community outreach initiatives. These experiences not only build social skills but also instill values of compassion, empathy, and a sense of belonging to a broader community.

Hosting playdates with other families offers an excellent opportunity for children to interact in a relaxed and comfortable setting. These gatherings can take place at homes, parks, or community centers, providing an environment for children to engage in imaginative play, develop social skills, and build friendships. The absence of rigid schedules allows homeschooling families to connect with others during weekdays, offering flexibility that traditional schooling may not provide.

It is also worth highlighting the significant role of sibling relationships in homeschooling socialization. Homeschooled children often have more opportunities to interact with their siblings throughout the day, fostering strong bonds and nurturing important social skills such as cooperation, conflict resolution, and empathy. These sibling relationships can provide a solid foundation for future interactions with peers and contribute to the development of well-rounded individuals.

It is important to remind critics that socialization is not solely limited to interacting solely with peers of the same age. In fact, homeschooling provides a unique environment where children can engage with individuals of different ages, backgrounds, and perspectives. They have the opportunity to interact with adults, siblings, younger children, and members of the broader community, gaining a more comprehensive understanding of the world around them.

As homeschooling parents, you have the freedom to curate a socialization experience that aligns with your family's values and priorities. By actively seeking out and embracing these diverse avenues for social interaction, you ensure that your children have a well-rounded social life that nurtures their emotional intelligence, empathy, and adaptability.

The misconception that homeschooling isolates children from social interactions is unfounded. Homeschooling families have a myriad of options for socialization, from extracurricular activities to homeschooling groups, community engagement, sibling relationships, and playdates. By actively participating in these activities, homeschooled children develop strong social skills, form meaningful connections, and thrive in a diverse social landscape. You can remind critics that socialization is not limited to interactions with peers of the same age but consists of a vast array of experiences that contribute to the holistic development of children.

But... You're Not a Teacher

Dealing with this outside pressure can be one of the greatest challenges in homeschooling. You may encounter individuals who believe that you are not educated enough to teach your own children. Their doubts and skepticism can create self-doubt within you. It's crucial to remember that you have made a thoughtful decision based on your own beliefs, values, and abilities. Trust in yourself and your capacity to provide an enriching educational experience for your children.

At times, you may encounter individuals who question your children's abilities or knowledge through quizzes or comparisons with other children. It's essential to resist the temptation to compare your children's achievements with those of others. Each child develops at their own pace and has their own strengths and talents. This is one of the values of homeschooling that you can focus on nurturing their individual growth rather than trying to match someone else's standards.

There will be those who silently observe your homeschooling journey and pass judgment without offering constructive feedback. Their comments may hint at their perception of your supposed failure. These external pressures can sometimes sow seeds of self-doubt within you. It's important to recognize that everyone's journey is unique, and what works for one family may not work for another. Remind yourself that you are making the best choices for your children and that their progress and growth are what truly matter.

I remember a dear friend of mine who initially intended to follow the traditional school route for her children. They enrolled in kindergarten, but it became evident that it wasn't the right fit for their family. Despite the resistance from her family, she made the courageous choice to embark on the homeschooling journey. However, challenges arose within the dynamics of her children. The younger sister often felt overshadowed by her older sibling, creating a sense of competition between them. Recognizing the need for resolution, my friend took proactive steps by researching and participating in communication courses. This process became an opportunity for the entire family to grow and learn how to communicate with compassion and understanding.

In the face of external judgments, it's important to hold onto the belief that you have made a thoughtful decision based on your own beliefs, values, and abilities. Trust in yourself and your capacity to provide an enriching educational experience for your children. Remember that each family's journey is unique, and what works for others may not necessarily work for you. Embrace the choices you have made and prioritize the progress and growth of your children above all else. This is also your opportunity to be flexible and adjust when you see something is not quite working the way you thought it would.

While criticisms may still arise, find solace in the knowledge that you are doing what you believe is best for your family. Surround yourself with a supportive network of like-minded individuals who can offer encouragement and guidance. Ultimately, the success of your homeschooling journey is measured by the positive impact it has on your children's education and overall well-being.

Self-Doubt, Your Own Worst Enemy

In the vast landscape of homeschooling, self-doubt may emerge as a persistent companion on your journey. It's natural to question yourself and wonder if you are doing enough or if you are doing it right. This internal dialogue can sometimes cloud your confidence and cast shadows of uncertainty. However, it's important to recognize that self-doubt is a normal part of the process and doesn't diminish your abilities as an educator and a parent.

During moments of self-doubt, it can be incredibly powerful to revisit your WHY—the deep-seated reasons that motivated you to embark on the homeschooling path in the first place. Perhaps you wanted to create a personalized learning experience that aligns with your family's values and priorities. Maybe you wanted to provide your children with a safe and nurturing environment where they can thrive academically, emotionally, and socially. Reflect on these motivations and remind yourself of the remarkable journey you have undertaken.

Take a moment to pause and look back at how far you and your children have come. Celebrate their achievements, both big and small. It's easy to overlook the progress when you are immersed in the day-to-day activities of homeschooling. But by intentionally reflecting on the growth, you will witness the transformative impact of your dedication and hard work.

Think about the knowledge your children have gained, the skills they have developed and the moments of inspiration and joy they have experienced. Consider the unique opportunities they have had to explore their interests, delve into subjects they are passionate about, and embrace a love for learning. These milestones are a testament to the positive influence you are having on their educational journey.

When self-doubt creeps in, remember that learning is a dynamic and evolving process. It's not solely about ticking off boxes or adhering to rigid standards. Homeschooling allows you the freedom to tailor the educational experience to the unique needs and learning styles of your children. Embrace the flexibility and adaptability homeschooling has to offer, allowing you to create an environment that fosters curiosity, creativity and a lifelong love for learning.

Another way to keep the negative thought away is to reach out to fellow homeschooling parents or support groups for encouragement and reassurance. Share your concerns and insecurities, and you will likely discover that many others have experienced similar moments of self-doubt. Engaging in conversations with like-minded individuals can provide invaluable insights, practical tips, and a sense of camaraderie that bolsters your confidence.

Remember, self-doubt is a reminder that you care deeply about your children's education. It shows your commitment to their growth and your desire to provide them with the best possible educational experience. Embrace the journey of self-discovery and growth, both for yourself and your children.

As you navigate the homeschooling terrain, keep in mind that there will be challenges and setbacks along the way. But that is how life works in general. However, your resilience and unwavering belief in your capabilities will allow you to overcome these obstacles. Embrace the opportunity to learn and grow alongside your children, knowing that you are providing them with a solid foundation for their future endeavors.

By overcoming self-doubt, you not only empower yourself as a homeschooling parent but also create an environment where your children can develop confidence in their own abilities. Together, you will continue to forge a path of learning, exploration, and personal growth, knowing that your decision to homeschool is rooted in love, dedication, and the pursuit of a remarkable educational journey.

Understanding Others' Perspectives

It's important to recognize that family, friends, and other individuals who offer criticism may not fully understand your perspective and the unique dynamics of homeschooling. They may view education as a structured environment with classrooms, bells, and uniforms, where learning is confined to a specific time and place. It's important to recognize that their concerns or comments may stem from a place of genuine concern or love for your children's well-being.

Empathy plays a vital role in navigating these conversations and understanding others' perspectives. Put yourself in their shoes and try to grasp their viewpoint, even if it differs from your own. Consider the context in which they formed their opinions and the assumptions they may hold about homeschooling. By doing so, you can approach discussions with a sense of compassion and openness, fostering a more constructive dialogue.

While it is natural to seek validation and understanding from others, it is equally important to accept that they may never fully grasp your point of view. Your homeschooling journey is deeply personal, driven by your family's deeply-held beliefs and values. Remember that you have made a deliberate and thoughtful decision to educate your children at home based on your knowledge of their unique needs and aspirations. Your conviction and dedication to providing them with the best educational experience should be your guiding light.

Instead of feeling discouraged or defensive when faced with criticism or misunderstanding, use it as an opportunity to share your perspective and educate others about the benefits and values of homeschooling. You can have conversations, providing insights into the flexibility, tailored curriculum, and individualized attention that homeschooling can offer. Share anecdotes and examples of how homeschooling has positively impacted your children's learning, growth, and overall well-being. By sharing your experiences, you can help others gain a deeper understanding of homeschooling as a viable and enriching educational option. Keep in mind that your goal is not to convince or convert but rather to broaden their perspective and foster a more informed dialogue.

It is essential to prioritize the clarity and confidence of your own convictions over seeking external validation. Trust your instincts as a parent and educator, knowing that you are making the best choices for your children's education. Embrace the fact that your journey is unique, tailored to your family's values, aspirations, and priorities. Your commitment to homeschooling is driven by a deep belief in the power of individualized education and the potential for your children to thrive in an environment that celebrates their uniqueness.

Remember that your homeschooling journey is an ongoing process of growth and learning, not just for your children but also for yourself. As you continue to explore and refine your approach to homeschooling, your confidence will grow, and your ability to address criticisms and misconceptions will strengthen. Embrace the opportunity to learn from others, but also trust in your own expertise and intuition as you navigate the path of homeschooling.

Lastly, understanding others' perspectives is essential in dealing with criticism and misconceptions about homeschooling. By empathizing with their limited viewpoint, engaging in meaningful conversations, and sharing your experiences, you can foster a deeper understanding of homeschooling's benefits and values. Ultimately, trust in your own convictions, as your journey is driven by your family's unique beliefs and values, creating an educational experience that aligns with your children's needs and aspirations.

Your WHY must remain strong and unwavering. You cannot change the opinions of others, and they will often assert their belief that you are wrong. If you choose to engage in debates about homeschooling, do so with confidence and gratitude for the opportunity to share your experiences and insights. However, it is equally important to accept that not everyone will understand or agree with your choices. Embrace your journey, stay focused on your purpose, and do not allow external criticisms to undermine your confidence.

Remember, critics will always be present in your life, regardless of your chosen path. However, remain steadfast in your convictions and remember why you have chosen homeschooling. Keep in mind that your homeschooling experience will always look different from a conventional school setup, making it challenging for others to fully grasp what it entails. Avoid comparing your children's progress to that of traditionally-schooled children, as your focus should be on their individual growth and development.

Now that we've covered some of the potential adversities you may encounter, I would like you to consider the questions below. By answering these questions, you can gain a deeper understanding of your own thoughts, worries, considerations, and perspectives related to dealing with criticisms and misconceptions in homeschooling.

What specific criticisms or doubts are you most concerned about hearing from others regarding your choice to homeschool?

_____

_____

_____

_____

How do you plan to respond to these criticisms?

_____

_____

_____

_____

How will you handle criticisms that are not directly voiced but rather hinted at?

_____

_____

_____

_____

Reflect on moments of self-doubt you have experienced on your homeschooling journey. How can you revisit your initial motivations for homeschooling and celebrate the progress and achievements of both yourself and your children?

_____

_____

_____

_____

How can you approach discussions with a sense of empathy, compassion, and openness?

_____

_____

_____

_____

How can you educate others about the benefits and values of homeschooling without trying to convince or convert them?

_____

_____

_____

_____

Reflect on the uniqueness of your homeschooling journey, tailored to your family's values, aspirations, and priorities. How can you maintain a clear vision of your homeschooling journey and stay focused on your purpose despite external criticisms and doubts?

_____

_____

_____

_____

How do you handle comparisons between your homeschooling experience and a conventional school setup? How can you avoid comparing your children's progress to that of traditionally-schooled children and instead focus on their individual growth and development?

_____

_____

_____

_____

By embracing your giants and confidently addressing criticisms, you can strengthen your resolve and maintain a clear vision of your homeschooling journey. Your commitment to your children's education, coupled with your understanding of the unique benefits of homeschooling, will empower you to overcome doubts and external pressures.

Four

Navigating the Legal Landscape of Homeschooling

It's important to understand your legal responsibilities before you start homeschooling. While this chapter provides general advice and is not country-specific, it aims to guide you in finding the necessary information regarding homeschooling regulations in your region. By knowing what to expect and where to seek legal guidance, you can navigate the process with confidence and peace of mind.

It's important to note that local schools may not be the best source of information when it comes to homeschooling legalities. They often lack comprehensive knowledge of homeschooling regulations, and their interests may not align with supporting homeschooling as an alternative option. However, if you are withdrawing your child from a traditional school, it may be appropriate to discuss the process with the school administration. They may require an official letter or documentation for legal purposes, and it's essential to fulfill any necessary obligations.

One of the initial questions that may arise is whether homeschooling is legal in your country. The legality of homeschooling varies across jurisdictions, and it's crucial to familiarize yourself with the specific laws and regulations applicable to your region. Researching educational laws and policies at the national, state, or provincial level can provide valuable insights into the legal status of homeschooling. Government websites, educational departments, or ministries of education often serve as reputable sources of information.

Additionally, you may inquire whether homeschooling requires registration or notification to the appropriate authorities. Some countries or regions may have specific processes in place, such as registering as a homeschooling family or submitting a notification of intent to homeschool. This step ensures that your homeschooling journey remains in compliance with legal requirements. Again, consult relevant government websites or educational departments to obtain accurate and up-to-date information on the registration process.

Another consideration is whether homeschooling is monitored or subject to oversight. Certain jurisdictions may have mechanisms in place to assess homeschooling programs or conduct periodic evaluations of students' progress. Understanding the extent and nature of any monitoring can help you align your homeschooling practices accordingly. Inquire about reporting requirements, assessment procedures, or any other forms of evaluation that may be expected of homeschooling families, and create a calendar around these important dates and milestones.

While delving into the legal aspects of homeschooling may initially seem overwhelming or even intimidating, it's important to remember that knowledge is power. By arming yourself with accurate information and understanding your legal obligations, you can confidently pursue homeschooling for your children. The resources available to you may include educational advocacy organizations, homeschooling associations, or online communities specific to your country or region. These platforms often provide comprehensive information, legal guidance, and support for homeschooling families.

Additionally, online forums or discussion groups comprising experienced homeschoolers in your locality can offer valuable insights and firsthand experiences regarding the legal landscape. Engaging with fellow homeschoolers can help you navigate any legal challenges, gain practical advice, and find reassurance in knowing that you are not alone on this journey.

Remember that laws and regulations surrounding homeschooling are subject to change. It's essential to stay informed and regularly check for updates or amendments to ensure ongoing compliance. By proactively seeking information, connecting with relevant resources, and remaining aware of your legal obligations, you can confidently embrace homeschooling within the framework of the law.

Now, let's take a moment to reflect on some key questions you should ask yourself to ensure ongoing compliance and confidently navigate the legal landscape of homeschooling.

Is homeschooling legal in your country or region? Are there any specific laws or regulations that govern homeschooling?

_____

_____

_____

_____

What are the specific local requirements and processes involved in the registration/notification as a homeschooling family?

_____

_____

_____

_____

Are there any monitoring or oversight mechanisms in place for homeschooling? Do you need to report on your child's progress or participate in assessments or evaluations?

_____

_____

_____

_____

How can you align your homeschooling practices with the requirements?

_____

_____

_____

_____

What resources are available to you for legal guidance and support? Are there educational advocacy organizations, homeschooling associations, or online communities specific to your country or region that you can reach out to?

_____

_____

_____

_____

How can you stay informed about any updates or amendments to homeschooling laws and regulations? What steps can you take to ensure ongoing compliance with the legal framework?

_____

_____

_____

_____

These questions address the key aspects of understanding the legal landscape of homeschooling, including legality, registration/notification, monitoring/oversight, available resources for support, and staying informed about legal updates. By finding answers to these questions, you can ensure you are complying with the law and confidently navigate the legal aspects of homeschooling as a homeschooling parent.

In the next chapter, we will delve into the various homeschooling approaches and methodologies, allowing you to choose a style that aligns with your family's educational philosophy and goals.

Five

Exploring Homeschooling Styles and Finding Your Fit

I have a question for you, have you already begun to think about which personalized approach to homeschooling aligns with your family's values, goals, and interests? If not, that's okay too. In this chapter, we will delve into practical questions and suggestions to help you assess which homeschooling style will work best for your family. By considering your family's unique needs, preferences, and circumstances, you can choose an approach that aligns with your educational philosophy and lifestyle. We will explore different homeschooling styles and provide suggestions on how certain family dynamics and schooling types could be a good fit.

Finding the right homeschooling style is about aligning your family's unique needs and preferences with an approach that resonates with your educational values. It's not about adhering to a rigid system or replicating someone else's method. Instead, it's a journey of self-discovery, where you have the freedom to adapt and personalize your approach to best serve your family.

Throughout this chapter, we will explore various homeschooling styles, such as classical education, Charlotte Mason, unschooling, and more. We will discuss each style's core principles, teaching methods, and potential benefits. It's important to remember that there is no one-size-fits-all approach, and you have the flexibility to blend and adapt different styles to create a unique homeschooling experience that meets your family's needs.

As you navigate the different homeschooling styles and reflect on your family's dynamics, remember to embrace experimentation and flexibility. Homeschooling is a dynamic and evolving process, and it's okay to make adjustments along the way. What works for one family may not work for another, and that's perfectly fine. Your homeschooling journey is an opportunity to explore, learn, and grow together as a family.

So, as we explore homeschooling styles, keep an open mind and trust your instincts. Listen to your children's needs, observe their interests, and stay true to your family's values and goals. By finding the homeschooling style that resonates with your family, you can create an educational experience that nurtures curiosity, fosters growth, and ignites a lifelong love for learning.

Taking this journey of self-discovery requires asking yourself important questions while keeping your family's collective needs and individual personalities in mind. In the following sections, we will delve deeper into these essential questions to consider when exploring homeschooling styles. By reflecting on your family's unique needs and dynamics and seeking clarity through these questions, you will be empowered to make informed decisions about the best approach to homeschooling for your family's educational journey.

- When is your best time of the day to work?

Consider the optimal time for both you and your children to engage in focused learning activities. Some families thrive in the morning, while others prefer afternoons or evenings. Identifying these peak productivity periods can help structure your daily routine effectively. Maybe it's not clear to you yet what the answer is, then give yourselves some time to experiment with different options.

Take into account each family member's preferences and individual learning styles. Some children may be early birds, eager to dive into their studies as soon as they wake up, while others may need a bit of time to ease into the day. Similarly, you might discover that you are more alert and focused during specific times of the day. By aligning your homeschooling schedule with these natural rhythms, you can create an environment that optimizes learning and engagement.

Consider the external factors that may influence your preferred work time as well. Are there any other commitments or activities that your family participates in regularly? Take into account extracurricular activities, appointments, or other obligations when determining the best time for focused homeschooling. This will help you strike a balance between academic pursuits and other aspects of life.

Keep in mind that flexibility is one of the advantages of homeschooling. While establishing a routine can help with consistency, it's also important to be adaptable. Life happens, and unexpected events or circumstances may disrupt your ideal schedule. Embrace the flexibility that homeschooling offers, and be open to adjusting your work time as needed. This flexibility can help you accommodate special projects, field trips, or spontaneous learning opportunities that arise.

Remember, finding the best time to work is a personal decision that will vary for each family. It's all about discovering what works best for you and your children. By considering everyone's energy levels, individual preferences, and external commitments, you can create a homeschooling schedule that promotes productivity, engagement, and enjoyment.

- Can you teach all your kids at the same time?

Assess whether your children are in similar grade levels or if there's a significant age gap that requires separate instruction. Depending on their needs, you may choose to combine subjects or tailor lessons to individualize their education.

Assessing whether you can teach all your children at the same time is an important consideration. Take into account their grade levels and any significant age gaps that may require separate instruction. Depending on their individual needs, you can choose to combine subjects or tailor lessons to provide a personalized education.

Let me share a story about a friend's experience with homeschooling. Her son initially struggled with anxiety and social settings when he attended school for a few months. Recognizing his need for a more supportive environment, they made the decision to homeschool him. In the beginning, his progress in reading was slow, and his mother patiently worked with him to learn to read in their home language. However, the following year, he surprised everyone by teaching himself how to read English (his second language).

His younger sister, who was present during all the lessons, absorbed much of the material and quickly mastered it when it was her turn to "do the learning." From a young age, this boy and his father spent countless hours working with computers, fixing them, taking them apart, and programming. Although math was always a struggle for him, his mother persevered with different approaches until he eventually grasped it.

Despite the challenges, he excelled in computer programming at a young age and is now thriving in his chosen university degree. Additionally, he developed a keen interest in learning Japanese and taught himself to communicate with fellow online gamers. Years later, he even wrote a Japanese exam and took a memorable road trip across Japan with his father.

As for his younger sister, she found her own path. She began volunteering at a kindergarten in a low-income area and inspired her friends to get involved as well. Throughout the years, she pursued her love for dancing, and her friends joined her in organizing a play that included dance items. The proceeds from the play were then donated to the kindergarten, demonstrating her commitment to making a positive impact.

Recently, she made the decision to become a midwife and has scheduled an internship at a local maternity hospital to gain firsthand experience.

This story serves as a reminder that homeschooling allows for the flexibility to meet each child's unique interests, strengths, and aspirations. It showcases how homeschooling can provide the space and opportunity for children to excel in their chosen fields and make meaningful contributions to their communities.

- Do you have a job?

If you are balancing homeschooling with work responsibilities, it's important to consider how your job will fit into your daily routine. Determine the amount of time you need to set aside for work and explore strategies for managing both roles effectively.

If you are juggling homeschooling with work responsibilities, finding a balance between the two is crucial. Consider how your job will fit into your daily routine and allocate dedicated time for work while ensuring you can devote quality time to your children's education.

I can relate to this struggle personally. I remember starting a business that I planned to run from home while simultaneously teaching my children during "off time." However, I soon realized that the nature of my business didn't allow me to block off specific hours for homeschooling. The demands of clients and projects took precedence, leaving little predictable time for focused teaching. The constant unpredictability caused stress, and I often felt overwhelmed, believing that I wasn't trying hard enough.

Upon reflection, I recognized that the type of business I had was not conducive to a balanced homeschooling journey. I had failed to anticipate the daily demands and time requirements that my business would entail. It became evident that I needed a different approach that would allow me to dedicate consistent and uninterrupted time to my children's education.

This realization is crucial for anyone considering homeschooling while managing work commitments. It's essential to assess your work situation and honestly evaluate whether you can allocate quality time for your children during designated school hours. Understanding the demands of your job and how it aligns with your homeschooling goals will help you make informed decisions and create a more sustainable routine.

Remember, homeschooling is a significant commitment that requires dedicated time and attention. By carefully considering your work situation and its compatibility with homeschooling, you can find a balance that allows you to meet both your professional and educational responsibilities effectively.

- Where will homeschooling take place?

Creating a productive learning environment is crucial for both children and parents. Consider the physical space available in your home and how it can be optimized for homeschooling. Ensure it meets the needs of your children's learning styles and accommodates your own workspace requirements.

When considering homeschooling, it's important to establish a conducive learning environment that fosters productivity and engagement for both you and your children. Assess the physical space available in your home and explore ways to optimize it for homeschooling, ensuring it caters to your children's learning styles and accommodates your own workspace needs.

I vividly recall a conversation I had with a dear friend when the idea of homeschooling was still new to me. She offered valuable insights into what a typical homeschooling and workday would look like, prompting me to envision how I could incorporate "school-like activities" into my daily schedule. Inspired by her advice, I decided to prioritize consistent reading time with my children.

We created a cozy reading spot beneath the shade of a tree, where a bench provided a comfortable seating area. Surrounded by nature, we immersed ourselves in captivating books, and as I read aloud, my children eagerly recited passages they had memorized. Occasionally, they would dangle from the tree branches, infusing our reading sessions with playful joy. Even to this day, snuggling up together and sharing the magic of storytelling remains a cherished tradition in our homeschooling journey.

This story highlights the significance of creating a learning environment that resonates with your family's values and preferences. It doesn't have to be a conventional classroom setting but rather a space that encourages curiosity, comfort, and connection. Whether it's a dedicated homeschooling room, a cozy reading nook, or a multifunctional area that adapts to various learning activities, the key is to establish an environment that cultivates engagement and inspires a love for learning.

By thoughtfully crafting a physical space that reflects the unique dynamics of your homeschooling journey, you can set the stage for meaningful educational experiences and create lasting memories with your children.

- What other activities need to be part of the schedule?

Besides academic subjects, factor in extracurricular activities, hobbies, sports, or social engagements that are important to your family. Balancing these activities with homeschooling can create a well-rounded educational experience.

As you craft your homeschooling schedule, it's crucial to consider the diverse range of activities that contribute to a well-rounded educational experience. Beyond academic subjects, think about incorporating extracurricular pursuits, hobbies, sports, and social engagements that hold significance for your family.

Let me share a personal dream that has sparked excitement and learning within our homeschooling journey. I've always wanted to take a road trip with our children, exploring the different corners of our country and immersing ourselves in its unique culture, landscapes, and history. It's an adventure that would not only provide educational opportunities but also create lasting memories together. Homeschooling allows us the freedom to plan such adventures and integrate them into our educational routine.

Maybe you also have a yearning for something beyond the traditional classroom. Is there a passion or curiosity that pulls at your heart, urging you to incorporate it into your homeschooling lifestyle? It could be anything from scientific exploration to artistic pursuits or engaging in community service. Embracing these passions and weaving them into your schedule can bring excitement, purpose, and depth to your homeschooling experience.

By giving importance to these additional activities alongside academic studies, you provide a well-rounded education that nurtures your children's minds, bodies, and spirits. Through these diverse experiences, children develop a broader perspective, discover their passions, and cultivate a lifelong love for learning.

As you embark on this homeschooling journey, allow yourself the freedom to dream and explore the possibilities that align with your family's values and aspirations. Homeschooling empowers you to embrace these dreams, whether it's navigating a road trip, immersing yourselves in a new language and culture, or engaging in any other extraordinary endeavor that ignites a spark within your family.

So, what experiences and adventures are calling you? Take a moment to envision the possibilities and consider how they can be part of your homeschooling schedule, enriching the educational tapestry of your family's journey. Let your imagination guide you as you create a homeschooling experience that is uniquely tailored to your family's passions and aspirations.

- How much time do you want to spend on schooling?

Consider the desired daily and weekly schedule for homeschooling. When it comes to the amount of time dedicated to homeschooling, every family has its own preferences and needs. Some prefer a structured approach with set hours, while others find a more flexible routine that allows for exploration and self-paced learning to be the best fit.

In our family, we have found that a routine-based schedule works well for us. I used to resist routines, believing that they took away the spontaneity and freedom in life. However, my perspective has shifted over time. I've come to realize that it's not about blindly following someone else's routine but rather creating our own path. This approach has brought a sense of balance and harmony to our homeschooling journey.

That being said, we also embrace the beauty of its flexibility. Sometimes, we let the weather guide our plans, deciding to go for a hike or a cycle and then dive into our schoolwork later that day. Other times, we take our books to a cozy coffee shop for a change of scenery. This is not a weekly occurrence, but we all find joy in the change of scenery from time to time. We also make it a point to organize outings with other homeschoolers, fostering social connections and shared experiences.

While I initially felt the pressure to do it all on my own, I've also learned the value of seeking support. Currently, my children attend a homeschooling center once a week, where they benefit from additional guidance and interaction with peers. This has been a valuable resource for us, reminding me that I don't have to shoulder the entire homeschooling journey alone.

Finding the right balance between structure and flexibility is an ongoing process for our family. It's about listening to everyone's needs and finding a middle ground that accommodates each individual while fostering a sense of togetherness. Through this journey, I'm constantly learning how to strike that balance and create a homeschooling experience that truly meets our family's unique needs and aspirations.

- Personality of family members

Take into account the unique personalities and learning styles of each family member. Some children may thrive in a structured environment, while others may flourish with more autonomy, creativity, and flexibility in their learning. As you assess your children's personalities and learning styles, also take into account your own teaching style. Consider how your approach aligns with their needs and preferences. Remember, homeschooling is not just about providing an education; it's about fostering a positive and supportive learning environment. And don't forget to prioritize self-care and filling your own cup first! Taking care of yourself as an educator and parent will ensure that you have the energy and enthusiasm to support your children's educational journey.

- Skill set of the kids and yourself

Reflect on your children's existing skills and talents. Identify areas where they excel and display natural abilities. These areas can be nurtured and further developed through a curriculum that aligns with their strengths and interests. Additionally, consider areas where they may require additional support or focus. Homeschooling provides a unique opportunity to tailor the educational experience to address specific challenges and provide targeted support. Similarly, take a moment to reflect on your own strengths as an educator. What skills or knowledge do you bring to the table? How can you leverage your expertise to facilitate your children's learning? Recognizing and utilizing your own strengths will not only enhance your effectiveness as a teacher but also create a more fulfilling and enriching homeschooling experience for your children. Remember, homeschooling is a collaborative journey where both you and your children will continue to learn and grow together.

Homeschooling Styles

Next up, let's explore different homeschooling styles and approaches that you may find appealing. It's important to note that these are just a few examples, and there are many variations and combinations to suit individual preferences.

- Traditional Homeschooling

One popular homeschooling style is traditional homeschooling, which draws inspiration from the structure and routines of traditional classroom settings. In this approach, you, as the primary teacher, assume the responsibility of delivering instruction and guiding your children through a structured curriculum. This approach focuses on core subjects such as math, science, language arts, and social studies, following a set schedule that mirrors the format of a traditional school environment.

However, traditional homeschooling also allows for flexibility and customization. While core subjects are emphasized, you have the freedom to incorporate additional subjects that align with your family's values and your child's interests. Whether it's art, music, entrepreneurship, or any other topic that you deem important to their growth and development, traditional homeschooling can be adapted to include a well-rounded and comprehensive curriculum.

One of the benefits of traditional homeschooling is the sense of familiarity and routine it provides. If you and your children thrive in structured environments, this style offers a framework that mimics a traditional educational setting, providing a sense of comfort and familiarity within the comforts of your own home.

Within the structure of traditional homeschooling, you have the opportunity to create a routine that suits your family's needs and lifestyle. You can set clear daily schedules, establish specific study times for different subjects, and create a sense of predictability that helps children thrive in their learning journey. This routine can bring a sense of stability and security to your homeschooling experience, ensuring that learning is consistent and progress is made in each subject area.

It's important to remember that while traditional homeschooling offers structure, it doesn't mean you have to adhere strictly to the traditional school model. Homeschooling allows for flexibility, and you have the freedom to adapt the curriculum, teaching methods, and resources to suit your child's individual learning style and interests. You can tailor the pace of instruction, explore alternative teaching methods, and incorporate hands-on activities or real-life experiences to make the learning process engaging and meaningful.

Ultimately, traditional homeschooling provides a well-established and proven framework for delivering instructions and guiding your child's education. It offers the benefits of structure, routine, and familiarity while still allowing for customization and adaptability. By combining the core subjects with additional topics that resonate with your family, you can create a comprehensive and enriching educational experience within the comfort of your own home.

- Online Learning

In the digital age we now live in, online learning has become an increasingly popular and effective homeschooling style. With the numerous advancements in technology, online learning harnesses the power of various digital platforms and resources to create virtual classrooms, interactive lessons, and educational websites. This style offers a vast array of online resources that cover a wide range of subjects, providing children with the opportunity to explore diverse topics and engage with interactive learning materials.

One of the significant advantages of most online learning is its flexibility in scheduling. Unlike traditional homeschooling or classroom-based learning, online learning allows children to learn at their own pace and on a timetable that suits their individual needs. This flexibility enables families to tailor the learning experience to fit their unique circumstances, accommodating various schedules and personal preferences. Whether your child is an early riser, a night owl, or prefers shorter bursts of focused learning, online learning can provide the freedom to adapt the schedule to their optimal learning times.

Another advantage of online learning is the abundance of digital resources available. Reputable online platforms and resources offer comprehensive curricula that align with your educational goals. These platforms provide interactive lessons, engaging multimedia content, and opportunities for collaboration and engagement. They often incorporate features such as quizzes, interactive exercises, and discussion forums, allowing children to actively participate in the learning process and solidify their understanding of the concepts being taught.

Online learning also opens doors to a wealth of knowledge and diverse educational experiences. Children can delve deep into their areas of interest, accessing specialized courses, virtual field trips, and expert-led instructional videos. Whether it's exploring ancient civilizations, learning about marine biology, or mastering a musical instrument, the digital resources available in online learning can cater to your child's unique passions and curiosity.

When considering online learning, it's important to research and select reputable online platforms and resources that align with your educational goals and values. Look for platforms that have a track record of providing quality education, offer comprehensive curricula that cover the necessary subjects, and provide opportunities for collaboration and engagement. Read reviews, seek recommendations from other homeschooling families, and take advantage of trial periods or demo versions to ensure that the platform meets your expectations.

As with any homeschooling style, it's essential to find the right balance between online learning and other learning experiences. Online learning can be a valuable tool, but it could also be supplemented with hands-on activities, real-world experiences, and social interactions that can help to provide a well-rounded education. Engage with your child, monitor their progress, and maintain open communication to ensure that online learning remains a positive and enriching aspect of their homeschooling journey.

Online learning offers a dynamic and flexible homeschooling style that harnesses the power of technology and provides a vast array of resources and opportunities for children to explore and engage with educational content. By researching and selecting reputable online platforms, you can create a customized learning experience that aligns with your educational goals and provides your child with the flexibility and access to knowledge that online learning offers.

- Homeschooling Centers or Cottage Schools

Homeschooling Centers or Cottage Schools offer a unique and enriching homeschooling experience by bringing together a group of homeschooling families in a community-based setting. These schools serve as collaborative learning environments where resources, expertise, and teaching responsibilities are shared among the families involved. Some other Cottage schools have tutors who assists your children as necessary.

During a period of our own homeschooling journey, my husband had the opportunity to run a homeschooling center from our home. We witnessed how children can naturally and eagerly teach themselves when given the freedom to explore their interests and passions while still receiving guidance and support from the adults around them.

Homeschooling centers or cottage schools provide a unique environment where children can interact with their peers, develop social skills, and build lasting friendships. These communities foster a sense of camaraderie and belonging as families come together to support one another on their homeschooling journey. The connections made within these communities often extend beyond the academic realm and can develop into lifelong friendships for both children and parents alike.

One of the significant advantages of homeschooling centers or cottage schools is the opportunity for collaborative learning. In these settings, families can pool their resources and expertise, allowing children to benefit from a wider range of educational experiences. Different parents may excel in various subjects or have unique skills to share, creating a diverse and enriching learning environment. Children can learn from one another, collaborate on projects, and engage in group activities that foster teamwork and cooperation.

Furthermore, homeschooling centers or cottage schools often organize gatherings, field trips, and events, providing additional opportunities for socialization and community building. These activities can range from educational outings to cultural experiences, nature explorations, or creative workshops. By participating in these events, children have the chance to broaden their horizons, deepen their understanding of the world, and develop a sense of connection to their local community.

Joining a homeschooling center or cottage school can also alleviate some of the challenges that homeschooling parents may face, such as feeling overwhelmed or isolated. Being part of a supportive community allows parents to share their concerns, exchange ideas, and gain valuable insights from fellow homeschooling families who may have faced similar situations. This sense of camaraderie and support can be particularly beneficial during challenging times or when seeking guidance and advice on specific educational approaches or resources.

Homeschooling centers or cottage schools provide a collaborative and social learning environment for homeschooling families. By joining these communities, children have the opportunity to interact with their peers, develop social skills, and build lasting friendships. The pooling of resources, expertise, and teaching responsibilities creates a rich and diverse learning environment that enhances the homeschooling experience. Moreover, being part of a supportive community can provide homeschooling parents with invaluable support, guidance, and a sense of connection on their homeschooling journey.

- Relaxed Homeschooling

In the realm of homeschooling styles, relaxed homeschooling stands out for its emphasis on child-led learning and the freedom to explore individual interests and passions. With this approach, parents have the flexibility to choose curriculum materials that align with their child's unique needs and cater to their specific areas of curiosity.

A story that exemplifies the essence of relaxed homeschooling involves a young boy who had a burning desire to create his own "Music Video" production. This project became a significant part of their homeschooling activities, allowing the boy to unleash his creativity and passion for music. To make his vision a reality, he prepared a presentation for his parents, outlining the intricacies of the project and the budget required. Recognizing his enthusiasm and commitment, his parents granted him the necessary funds.

As the project progressed, challenges arose. Midway through, it became evident that the boy had overshot his budget. However, within the safe and supportive environment of homeschooling, the family found a way to overcome this hurdle. They made necessary compromises and added a bit of extra budget, enabling the successful completion of the music video. This experience not only fostered the boy's artistic expression but also taught him valuable lessons about budgeting, resourcefulness, and adapting to unexpected circumstances.

This story beautifully encapsulates the essence of relaxed homeschooling, where children are encouraged to pursue their passions and take ownership of their learning journeys. By providing the freedom to explore and support their interests, relaxed homeschooling empowers children to thrive academically, creatively, and personally. It demonstrates that within the homeschooling environment, children have the space and opportunity to bring their dreams to life, embracing the joy of learning while gaining essential life skills along the way.

It's important to acknowledge that finding the right homeschooling style can be a challenging process. There were times when my children resisted traditional sit-down class sessions, prompting us to experiment with different approaches. It took about six months before we established a daily schedule of work. During this period, I faced self-doubt, pressure from others, and unrealistic expectations of rapid progress. Patience became a valuable lesson as I learned to meet my children at their individual pace and avoid comparing them to their peers in conventional schooling.

Through the support of bloggers, friends, and teachers, I realized that every child has their own unique learning journey. Homeschooling allows us to tailor their education to their needs and progress at their own pace. It's important to remember that our children cannot be measured against traditional school standards because they aren't following the same path. Comparisons to their cousins or others their age only lead to self-doubt and unnecessary pressure.

As you explore homeschooling styles, keep in mind the individual needs, interests, and personalities of your children. Trust your intuition and be open to adjusting your approach as you discover what works best for your family. The beauty of homeschooling lies in its adaptability and the freedom to create a customized educational experience.

Take a moment and envision your homeschooling style and specifics, then answer the questions below.

When and where will your homeschooling take place?

_____

_____

_____

_____

How much time will you spend homeschooling each day/week?

_____

_____

_____

_____

What other activities do you want to include?

_____

_____

_____

_____

How do sibling relationships play a role in socialization within your homeschooling environment?

_____

_____

_____

_____

What homeschooling style or combination of styles resonated best with you?

_____

_____

_____

_____

Why do you feel this style is the best fit for your child(ren)?

_____

_____

_____

_____

Six

Choosing or Creating Your Own Homeschooling Curriculum

The process of choosing or creating a homeschooling curriculum may seem daunting and feel overwhelming at first, but with the right guidance and practical examples, it can become an exciting and rewarding endeavor. In this chapter, we will explore various steps to help you navigate through this process, ensuring that your curriculum aligns with your child's needs and your educational goals.

Research Your Local Homeschooling Regulations

Begin by familiarizing yourself with the homeschooling regulations in your state or country if you haven't done so already. This is a critical step to ensure a smooth homeschooling journey for you and your family. Familiarize yourself with the legal requirements and obligations that homeschooling families must meet. This step will help you understand the curriculum standards, reporting procedures, assessment requirements, and any other regulations you need to adhere to. By knowing and following these regulations, you can ensure that your homeschooling curriculum meets all necessary criteria and remains in compliance with the law.

This is like following a recipe to make a cake; all the steps must be followed in order, and the right ingredients must be used. Otherwise, the end result won't meet expectations. In the same way, if you don't meet the legal requirements for homeschooling, you may not get the desired outcomes.

Decide on a Homeschooling Method

Once you have a clear understanding of the legal landscape, it's time to explore the different homeschooling methods available. The various homeschooling types encompass numerous educational philosophies, teaching styles, and approaches to learning. Consider the diverse range of methods, including traditional approaches, online learning, Montessori, Waldorf, Charlotte Mason, and unschooling. Each type offers unique advantages and approaches to education. By considering your child's learning style and your own preferences, you can determine which method best suits your family's needs and values.

Traditional homeschooling, as mentioned earlier, follows a structured approach similar to a traditional school setting. It typically involves using textbooks and adhering to a predetermined curriculum. Online learning, on the other hand, utilizes digital platforms and resources to deliver interactive lessons and engage students in virtual classrooms. Montessori emphasizes hands-on learning, independent exploration, and self-paced progress. Waldorf education prioritizes artistic expression, imagination, and holistic development. Charlotte Mason emphasizes living books, nature study, and the cultivation of good habits. Unschooling promotes self-directed learning, allowing children to follow their interests and learn through real-life experiences.

When deciding on a homeschooling method, consider your child's learning style, interests, and strengths, as well as your own educational philosophy and teaching preferences. Reflect on the goals you have for your child's education and how each method aligns with those goals. Remember, you are not bound to a single method, and you can also combine elements from different methods to create a customized approach that suits your family's unique needs.

By carefully considering the different homeschooling methods and their underlying principles, you can choose an approach that resonates with your family's values and supports your child's individual learning journey. Keep in mind that flexibility is key, and you can always adapt and modify your chosen method as you gain experience and learn more about what works best for your child.

Choose Your Core Subjects

As you move forward, it's time to choose the core subjects that will be the foundation of your homeschooling curriculum. These subjects may include math, science, language arts, and social studies. However, remember that homeschooling allows for flexibility and creativity. Tailor your choices based on your child's interests, strengths, and future educational goals.

You can take a subject and explore it from various angles, allowing your child's curiosity to guide the learning process. For example, I have a cousin with 5 children. The eldest decided to delve deep into the world of guitars, exploring its history, science, construction, influential musicians, and more for a full year. In doing so, she learned to ask questions that lead to interesting facts. This approach encourages a love for learning and nurtures curiosity.

Moreover, it's important not to confine your curriculum solely to traditional academic subjects. Homeschooling opens the door to incorporating non-traditional areas of education, such as gardening, cooking, stock trading, financial literacy, or entrepreneurship. Personally, I held a vision of allowing my children to gain exposure to working environments before they embark on their future career paths. To fulfill this dream, my family embarked on a small handcrafting business venture. Our approach is driven by the belief that the profitability of the business is not the primary goal. Instead, we prioritize creating a learning environment with minimal risk, where my children can acquire diverse skills and, most importantly, have fun in the process. This approach instills the idea of embracing one's passions and finding joy in what they do. These exceptional experiences not only nurture practical knowledge but also encourage children to explore their interests, develop their true passions and chase some of their "wilder" dreams.

Set Learning Goals

To create a focused curriculum, establish clear learning goals for each subject. Break down these goals into specific objectives that will guide your curriculum planning. While this chapter provides some starter goals for core subjects like math, reading, writing, science, social studies, and music, you can tailor them to meet the specific needs and interests of your children.

- Math - Develop basic math skills and understanding of concepts like addition, subtraction, multiplication, division, fractions, decimals, shapes, and basic algebra.

- Reading - Increase reading comprehension, fluency, and understanding of phonemic awareness, word recognition, parts of speech, sentence structure, and story elements.

- Writing - Develop grammar, punctuation, and writing skills, including pre-writing, drafting, revising, and editing. Foster an understanding of narrative and other written expression forms.

- Science - Cultivate an understanding of scientific concepts, the scientific method, and physical, earth, and life sciences. Encourage problem-solving skills using the scientific process.

- Social Studies - Promote knowledge about geography, historical events, diverse cultures, and their global impact.

- Entrepreneurship - Develop an understanding of the fundamentals of starting and running a business. Foster a sense of curiosity for growing wealth through business opportunities.

- Music, Discovery, or Other - Develop skills in reading sheet music, comfort with finger placement, and note recognition. Encourage exploration of instrument and musical influence.

Choose Your Curriculum Resources

Selecting the right curriculum resources for your homeschooling journey requires thorough research and exploration. It is wise to gather information from various sources to determine the best fit for your family's unique needs. Consider the following avenues to conduct your research and find the expert voices that resonate with you.

Online Research

Utilize reputable websites to provide valuable insights and resources to support your curriculum choices. The websites below are examples that have been widely used and recognized in the homeschooling community offering a wealth of resources, curriculum options, and support for homeschooling families. However, it's always recommended to thoroughly research and evaluate the curriculum options to ensure they align with your family's educational goals and values.

- Khan Academy (www.khanacademy.org) - Khan Academy is a renowned online educational platform that provides free video lessons and interactive exercises across a wide range of subjects, including math, science, history, and more.

- Time4Learning (www.time4learning.com) - Time4Learning is a comprehensive online curriculum that covers core subjects such as math, language arts, science, and social studies. It offers interactive lessons, assessments, and progress-tracking tools.

- Oak Meadow (www.oakmeadow.com) - Oak Meadow offers a holistic, nature-based homeschooling curriculum for grades K-12. It focuses on experiential learning, creativity, and critical thinking.

- Calvert Homeschool (www.calverthomeschool.com) - Calvert Homeschool provides accredited curriculum and support for homeschooling families. Their materials cover core subjects and offer personalized learning options.

- AmblesideOnline (www.amblesideonline.org) - AmblesideOnline follows Charlotte Mason's educational philosophy and offers a free, book-based curriculum. It emphasizes living books, nature study, and the development of good habits.

- Sonlight (www.sonlight.com) - Sonlight offers literature-based curriculum packages for homeschooling families. Their materials incorporate quality literature and hands-on activities across various subjects.

- A Beka Academy (www.abeka.com) - A Beka Academy offers a Christian-based homeschooling curriculum with a strong emphasis on academic rigor. Their materials cover core subjects and are aligned with a traditional approach.

- Homeschool.com (www.homeschool.com) - Homeschool.com is a comprehensive resource website that provides information, articles, reviews, and a directory of homeschooling resources and curricula.

Seek Recommendations

Consult local public libraries, homeschooling groups, and experienced homeschooling parents for recommendations. Their firsthand experiences and knowledge can guide you in finding reliable and effective curriculum resources.

Engage in Online Communities

Participate in online forums, discussion boards, and social media platforms dedicated to homeschooling. Connect with experienced homeschoolers and educational organizations to gather insights, tips, and recommendations on curriculum options.

Attend Events and Workshops

Take advantage of homeschooling conventions, and workshops and seek guidance from homeschooling advisors. These events provide opportunities to explore a wide range of available resources and receive personalized advice from experts in the field.

By actively seeking information and engaging with different resources, you can make informed decisions and choose curriculum materials that align with your educational philosophy and meet your child's learning needs. Remember, the key is to find resources that resonate with your family's values and inspire a love for learning in your homeschooling journey.

Create a Schedule

Develop a weekly or monthly schedule for your homeschooling curriculum, considering your family's routine, breaks, and free time. Be sure you prioritize balance, flexibility, and alignment with your child's learning preferences and goals. Structuring a homeschooling journey is similar to building a house; you need to have a solid foundation with a clear plan and timeline, then add in the details like materials and activities that nurture your child's learning. If the foundation isn't strong, the whole project can crumble.

Choosing or creating your own homeschooling curriculum can be an empowering and fulfilling experience. By researching local regulations, selecting a suitable homeschooling method, setting clear learning goals, choosing appropriate resources, and creating a schedule, you can design a curriculum that caters to your child's individual needs and fosters a love for learning. Remember, this journey is unique to your family, and it's okay to evolve and make adjustments along the way. Embrace the process and enjoy the freedom that homeschooling provides in tailoring an education that suits your child's growth and development.

Answer the questions below will help you prepare and analyze the best curriculum suited for your family.

Which homeschooling method resonates with you and aligns with your child's learning style?

_____

_____

_____

_____

Which curriculum resources will you research?

_____

_____

_____

_____

What are the core subjects you want to prioritize in my homeschooling curriculum?

_____

_____

_____

_____

Have you established clear learning goals for each subject? Have you broken down these goals into specific objectives that will guide my curriculum planning?

_____

_____

_____

_____

What schedule will you set for your homeschooling curriculum that balances routine, and flexibility and aligns with your child's learning preferences and goals?

_____

_____

_____

_____

As you reflect upon these questions and embark on the journey of choosing or creating your own homeschooling curriculum, remember that you are not alone. The next chapter will delve into the topic of finding help and support along your homeschooling journey.

Whether it's connecting with local homeschooling groups, seeking guidance from experienced homeschoolers, or utilizing online resources and communities, there is a vast network of support available to you. By reaching out for assistance and building connections within the homeschooling community, you can find the help and encouragement you need to navigate any challenges that may arise. Embrace the opportunity to learn from others, share experiences, and grow together.

Seven

Finding Help – You Don't Have to Do It Alone

Being a homeschooler doesn't mean you have to handle all the duties and challenges all alone. In fact, seeking help and support can enhance the homeschooling experience for both you and your children. It's important to recognize that homeschooling doesn't have to be a solitary endeavor. Consider the numerous benefits of seeking assistance, whether it's through outsourcing certain aspects or connecting with homeschooling communities. By reaching out for assistance, you can tap into a wealth of resources, expertise, and community support.

Understand that the decision to outsource or seek help is a personal one, and there is no right or wrong answer. It's essential to assess your individual circumstances and determine when and how much you want to outsource. Every family is unique, and by exploring the possibilities, you can find the right balance that best supports your homeschooling journey. In this chapter, we will cover various avenues for finding help and support, whether it's through outsourcing certain aspects, connecting with homeschooling communities, involving friends and family, or utilizing online resources.

Outsourcing Options

When considering outsourcing, it's important to determine which aspects of homeschooling you may want to seek assistance with. Every family's needs and circumstances are unique, so take the time to assess what areas could benefit from additional support. This could range from specific subjects to extracurricular activities or even administrative tasks. Explore seasonal outsourcing options that allow for temporary assistance during specific periods or subjects. For example, you may choose to hire a tutor for a challenging math concept or enlist the help of a language instructor for foreign language learning. Additionally, consider in-person options such as joining homeschooling co-ops or groups where families come together to share teaching responsibilities or expertise in different subjects. These co-ops often provide a collaborative learning environment and opportunities for group projects or specialized classes. Furthermore, explore online resources and platforms that offer virtual classes, instructional videos, or live sessions. Many reputable online learning platforms cater specifically to homeschoolers and can provide comprehensive and interactive educational content.

Meeting with Other Homeschoolers

Joining homeschooling communities or support groups can be immensely beneficial for both you and your children. These communities provide opportunities to connect with other homeschooling families, exchange ideas, share experiences, and find inspiration. Regular meetups, gatherings, or field trips organized by these groups can foster a sense of camaraderie and provide valuable socialization opportunities for your children. Engaging with fellow homeschoolers allows you to build a support network and access a wealth of knowledge and resources. Seasoned homeschoolers can offer valuable insights and advice, recommending curriculum materials, sharing teaching strategies, and providing support during challenging times. Additionally, they may organize workshops or seminars where you can learn from experts in the field of homeschooling.

Bartering and Collaborating

Another creative way to find help is by exploring the possibility of bartering with other homeschooling families. Consider exchanging activities or subjects where one family may excel while another needs assistance. For example, if you have expertise in art, you could offer art lessons to another family in exchange for math tutoring for your child. Collaborating with a group of homeschoolers can also be an effective way to share resources and costs. By pooling together, you can hire a tutor or instructor for specific subjects, providing your children with specialized guidance while sharing the financial burden. Collaborative efforts like these create a sense of community and can lead to lasting friendships among homeschooling families.

Involving Family Members

If your family is supportive of homeschooling, consider involving them in the process. Grandparents, aunts, uncles, or older siblings can contribute their knowledge, skills, or time to enrich your child's learning experience. They may have expertise in certain subjects or hobbies that can be incorporated into your homeschooling curriculum. For example, a grandparent who is passionate about gardening could teach your child about plants, while an older sibling who excels in writing could provide feedback on their compositions. Involving family members not only brings a fresh perspective to the learning journey but also strengthens family bonds and creates cherished memories.

Online Resources and Virtual Learning

The digital age has provided an abundance of online resources and virtual learning opportunities for homeschoolers. Explore online schooling options that provide video lessons or live classes in various subjects. These programs often offer a structured curriculum, assessments, and progress-tracking tools. Additionally, utilize educational websites, platforms, and learning resources specifically designed for homeschoolers. These resources can provide interactive lessons, worksheets, educational games, and other engaging materials. To stay connected with the broader homeschooling community, follow homeschooling blogs, social media accounts, and forums. These platforms offer a wealth of information, advice, and support from experienced homeschoolers. Online support groups and virtual co-ops provide additional resources and opportunities for collaboration and shared learning experiences.

Adaptability and Experimentation

As you seek help and support in your homeschooling journey, embrace a mindset of adaptability and flexibility. Each family's needs and circumstances are unique, so it's important to experiment with different strategies, resources, and support systems to find what works best for you. Involve your children in the decision-making process, allowing them to observe and participate in finding the most suitable assistance. By fostering an environment of open-mindedness and adaptability, you can ensure that your homeschooling experience is tailored to meet the evolving needs of your family.

Remember, homeschooling doesn't mean you have to bear the entire burden alone. By seeking help and support, whether through outsourcing, connecting with homeschooling communities, involving friends and family, or utilizing online resources, you can enhance your homeschooling experience and provide your children with a broader range of educational opportunities. Embrace the idea of collaboration, adaptability, and experimentation, knowing that finding help is not a sign of weakness but a testament to your dedication to your child's education. Homeschooling is a journey best enjoyed with a supportive community by your side.

The questions below are designed to foster self-reflection, explore potential support systems, and contemplate adaptable approaches to homeschooling. They highlight the significance of involving children in the decision-making process to cultivate a positive and engaging learning environment. By addressing these questions, you can gain valuable insights into the benefits of seeking help and support, transforming your homeschooling journey into an enriching and enjoyable educational experience for your children. Take a moment to consider each question thoughtfully and respond with your unique perspectives and aspirations for your family's homeschooling adventure. I hope that your answers will guide you toward creating a supportive and thriving homeschooling community that nurtures a love for learning and fosters lasting memories for both you and your children.

Take some time to identify specific subjects, extracurricular activities, or administrative tasks that might be more effectively handled with external help. What aspects of homeschooling could benefit from outsourcing or additional support in your family's unique circumstances?

_____

_____

_____

_____

How do you envision your ideal homeschooling support network? Are you interested in joining homeschooling co-ops or support groups for collaborative learning opportunities and socialization? Alternatively, do you prefer online resources and virtual learning platforms to provide interactive educational content?

_____

_____

_____

_____

How do you plan to adapt and experiment with different strategies, resources, and support systems to find what works best for your family's unique needs?

_____

_____

_____

_____

What steps can you take to involve your children in the decision-making process to ensure their engagement and satisfaction with the assistance received?

_____

_____

_____

_____

Eight

Keep Track, Record, and Celebrate

As a homeschooling parent, one of the key responsibilities you have is to keep track of your child's progress and educational journey. It's not just about maintaining records for legal compliance but also about celebrating achievements, monitoring growth, and reflecting on the incredible milestones your child reaches. Let's explore the various aspects of keeping track and how it can enhance your homeschooling experience. We will start by addressing the initial hurdles you may encounter when it comes to tracking progress. From there, we will delve into the importance of tracking and provide you with practical ideas to help you navigate this journey with confidence.

The Initial Hurdle

Let's begin by tackling the initial hurdle and understanding the significance of keeping track of your homeschooling adventure. Personally, when we started our homeschooling journey, the idea of keeping track was overwhelming. As a parent, I didn't have the qualifications of a trained teacher with years of experience in planning and tracking. My focus was on simply providing the basic educational necessities for my children. However, as we gained clarity on our homeschooling goals and the direction we wanted to take, the importance of keeping track became evident. It became a tool to guide us toward our desired destination.

Keeping track of your child's progress is a crucial aspect of your homeschooling venture as their parent, teacher, and advocate. While it may initially seem daunting, especially if you don't have a background in education, it's important to recognize the importance of tracking and embrace it as an integral part of your homeschooling process. Tracking serves multiple purposes, including maintaining records for legal compliance, celebrating achievements, and monitoring your growth as a teacher.

It helps you maintain a sense of direction and ensures that you are on the right path to achieving your homeschooling goals. While tracking progress may not have initially seemed important to me as a parent, I now realize that it is equally beneficial for my personal growth as the "teacher." Seeing the progress my children make is incredibly motivating for both them and myself. It provides a tangible reminder of the impact of our efforts and encourages us to continue on this homeschooling path we are undergoing together.

At the beginning of your homeschooling voyage, you may encounter hurdles when it comes to keeping track of your child's progress. This is natural, especially if you are new to homeschooling or lack experience in traditional education settings. It's understandable to feel overwhelmed or unsure about where to start. However, as you gain clarity on your homeschooling goals and understand the unique needs of your child, you will realize that keeping track becomes increasingly important in guiding your progress.

By acknowledging the initial hurdle and recognizing the significance of tracking, you can overcome any hesitations and embark on a rewarding journey of monitoring your child's progress. Embrace the opportunity to stay organized, celebrate milestones, and identify areas that require further attention. Remember that tracking not only benefits your child but also contributes to your own growth as a homeschooling parent.

As you navigate through the homeschooling process, tracking progress will help you maintain a sense of direction and ensure that you are providing a comprehensive education for your child. It allows you to assess their development, tailor your teaching approach, and make informed decisions about their learning journey. Embrace the initial challenges, seek support from homeschooling communities, and explore practical tracking methods that work best for you and your child. By embracing the importance of tracking, you can confidently navigate your homeschooling adventure and create a meaningful educational experience for your child.

The Personal Benefits of Tracking

Keeping track of your child's progress is not only for external purposes, but it also offers numerous personal benefits for you as a homeschooling parent. Beyond the external benefits, such as fulfilling legal requirements, tracking progress holds personal benefits for both you and your children. It is not just about creating records; it is a tool for your own growth and development as a homeschooling parent. By documenting and tracking your child's learning journey, you create a tangible record of their progress, improvement, and milestones.

By tracking your child's progress, you can assess the effectiveness of your teaching methods, identify areas of improvement, and make informed decisions about your curriculum and instructional strategies. This record serves as a powerful tool for reflection and self-assessment, allowing you to identify areas of strength and areas that may need more focus. It allows you to reflect on your own teaching journey and adapt your approach to meet your child's needs better. As you witness the growth and development of your child, you gain a deeper understanding of their learning style, strengths, and areas for further exploration. This will help you to grow and see where you can improve and adapt to their preferred style.

Tracking progress also plays a vital role in recognizing and celebrating the accomplishments and milestones achieved by your child. It provides tangible evidence of their growth, improvement, and achievements, which can be a source of motivation and encouragement. When children see their progress visually represented, such as through completed assignments, projects, or portfolios, they gain a sense of accomplishment and pride in their learning journey. It reinforces their belief in their own abilities and fosters a love for learning.

Moreover, tracking progress serves as a powerful motivational tool for both you and your children. As you witness their progress and development, you are encouraged to continue providing quality education and nurturing their growth. For children, seeing their efforts and achievements documented helps them recognize their capabilities and motivates them to strive for further success. It instills a sense of responsibility and ownership of their learning, as they take pride in their accomplishments and understand the connection between effort and progress.

Also, you can seek help and include your child in tracking their own progress. Involving your child in the tracking process can be empowering and encourage their active engagement in their own education. Allow them to take ownership of their learning by setting goals, monitoring their progress, and reflecting on their achievements. This not only promotes a sense of responsibility and self-awareness but also enhances their critical thinking and metacognitive skills.

In addition to the practical and personal benefits, tracking progress can also be incredibly helpful for homeschooling parents in maintaining their sanity and managing their homeschooling journey effectively. As a homeschooling parent, you have numerous responsibilities on your plate, from planning lessons and teaching to managing household chores and other commitments. Keeping track of your child's progress allows you to stay organized and have a clear overview of their learning milestones and accomplishments. This knowledge helps you manage your time and resources more efficiently, ensuring that you can provide the necessary support and guidance when needed. By having a structured approach to tracking progress, you can alleviate stress and anxiety, knowing that you have a reliable system in place to monitor your child's educational journey. It provides a sense of reassurance and peace of mind, allowing you to focus on the joy of homeschooling and savor the precious moments spent with your child.

So, embrace the practice of tracking progress as a valuable tool not only for your child's education but also for your own well-being as a homeschooling parent.

When it comes to tracking progress, it's important to remember that it goes beyond traditional testing methods. While assessments can provide valuable insights, consider incorporating a variety of approaches to capture the full range of your child's learning and development. For instance, you can maintain portfolios showcasing their projects, artwork, and written assignments. Journaling or reflective exercises can help children express their thoughts and insights about their learning experiences. Observations, discussions, and checklists can also provide valuable information about their progress. Next, we'll look at some examples below of helpful and practical ideas to help monitor yourself and your child's progress and keep track of all you have (both!) accomplished.

Celebrate your child's achievements, monitor their growth, and reflect on your own development as a homeschooling parent. Let tracking progress serve as a powerful tool for motivation, reflection, and continuous improvement.

Practical Ideas for Keeping Track

When it comes to tracking progress, incorporating visual examples can be a powerful and engaging approach. Consider using charts, graphs, or portfolios to illustrate different methods of tracking.

- Charts and Graphs

Creating a visual chart or graph to track progress can be an engaging and effective way to monitor your child's growth. Consider using colorful charts or graphs that allow both you and your children to visually see the progress made in different subjects or areas of learning. Whether it's tracking reading milestones, math facts mastered, or science experiments completed, visual representations provide a clear snapshot of their achievements and motivate them to keep pushing forward.

- Spreadsheets and Recording Tools

Utilizing a spreadsheet or online tool is a practical and convenient method to maintain a record of grades, assignments completed, and overall progress. Online tools and spreadsheets provide an organized and easily accessible way to track and manage data. They allow you to input grades, track completed assignments, and generate progress reports when needed. These digital tools streamline the tracking process, saving you time and ensuring accurate record-keeping.

- Checklists or Calendars

Creating checklists or using calendars is a simple yet effective approach to keeping track of daily or weekly assignments. By creating checklists, you can monitor completed tasks, check off completed assignments, and plan future activities effectively. Calendars can be used to mark important due dates, schedule study sessions, and track progress over time. These tangible tools help you and your child stay organized and ensure that nothing falls through the cracks.

- Reward Systems

Implementing a reward system can motivate your children to stay focused and engaged in their learning. Consider using stickers, stars, or points to acknowledge achievements and encourage them to complete tasks or reach specific goals. You can create a reward chart where they earn points or stickers for completing assignments, demonstrating good behavior, or achieving milestones. This system adds an element of fun and excitement to the learning process, motivating your children to put forth their best effort.

- Photos

Capturing visual evidence of completed projects, artwork, or assignments is a creative way to document progress and showcase accomplishments. Take photos of your child's work and compile them in a portfolio. This portfolio can serve as a tangible record of their achievements and growth. It also allows you and your child to reflect on the progress they've made and provides a visual representation of their learning journey.

- Essays

Encouraging children to write reflections or essays about their learning experiences promotes self-assessment and a deeper understanding of the topics covered. Have them write short reflections after completing a project, reading a book, or participating in a science experiment. This reflective writing provides a valuable opportunity for them to express their thoughts, identify areas of growth, and gain a better understanding of their own learning process.

- Online Portfolio Platforms

Utilizing an online portfolio platform designed for homeschoolers can be a convenient way to store and showcase your children's work. These platforms offer features that allow you to create digital portfolios where you can upload and organize their assignments, projects, and artwork. Online portfolios can be easily accessed and shared with others, providing a comprehensive view of their educational journey.

- Journals

Maintaining a journal dedicated to your homeschooling experience allows you to record observations, milestones, challenges, and successes encountered along the way. This personal reflection tool serves as a source of inspiration and allows you to see how far you and your children have come. Use the journal to jot down memorable moments, reflect on breakthroughs, and brainstorm new ideas. It provides a space for self-reflection and a way to track your own growth as a homeschooling parent.

- Check-Ins

Setting aside regular time for check-ins with your children is a valuable practice in monitoring progress and fostering open communication. Schedule weekly or monthly check-ins where you can sit down with your children to review their progress, discuss challenges they may be facing, and set goals for the future. These check-ins provide an opportunity to celebrate achievements, address any concerns, and collaborate on the next steps in their learning journey. It also reinforces the idea that their education is a shared effort and that their voice and input matter.

Keeping track of your child's progress is an essential aspect of homeschooling that serves multiple purposes. It goes beyond mere record-keeping for legal compliance; it becomes a tool for celebration, monitoring progress, and reflection. By implementing practical tracking ideas that go beyond traditional testing methods, you can create a rich and meaningful record of your homeschooling experience.

By implementing these practical ideas for keeping track, you can effectively monitor your child's progress, celebrate their accomplishments, and make informed decisions about their educational journey. Choose the methods that resonate with you and your child, and remember that tracking progress is not only a means of record-keeping but also a tool for motivation, reflection, and growth.

As you explore different tracking methods, don't hesitate to look for online sources or mommy bloggers who have shared innovative and effective ideas. The homeschooling community is rich with resources, and many parents generously share their experiences and insights. Seek inspiration from those who have found creative ways to track progress and adapt their ideas to suit your own homeschooling journey. You can find blogs, websites, or social media accounts dedicated to homeschooling that offers a wealth of tracking ideas and inspiration. Remember to give credit where it's due and share your own experiences to contribute to the community.

Recognize the importance of tracking progress in staying organized and informed about your child's educational journey. It provides a sense of direction and accomplishment for both you and your children. Celebrate their achievements, big and small, and take pride in the progress they make. Use tracking as an opportunity to reflect on your growth as a homeschooling parent and make adjustments when necessary.

Be open-minded and adaptable as you explore different tracking methods and ideas. What works for one family may not work for another, and that's perfectly okay. The key is to find a tracking system that resonates with you and your child, one that is practical, engaging, and aligned with your educational philosophy. Remember that each child's journey is unique, and tracking progress allows you to tailor their education to their individual needs and interests. Engage your child in the tracking process, involving them in setting goals and assessing their own progress. This collaborative approach fosters a love for learning and a deeper engagement with education.

Embrace the journey of keeping track with enthusiasm and creativity. Make it a collaborative effort with your child and enjoy the fulfillment that comes from documenting their growth and development. Your dedication and commitment to tracking progress will not only provide a comprehensive record of your homeschooling experience but also foster a deeper appreciation for the incredible learning journey you and your children are undertaking together.

Below are a few questions that cover the importance, benefits, and practical aspects of tracking progress in homeschooling, as well as how to overcome challenges and make it a positive and enriching experience for both you and your child. Answering these questions will provide you with valuable insights and guidance in effectively tracking your child's educational journey.

What are the initial hurdles you anticipate facing or challenges you may encounter when it comes to tracking your child's progress in homeschooling?

_____

_____

_____

_____

How can keeping track of your child's progress benefit both you as a homeschooling parent and your child's learning journey?

_____

_____

_____

_____

In what ways can you involve your child in the tracking process to encourage their active engagement in their own education?

_____

_____

_____

_____

How can you incorporate visual examples, such as charts, graphs, or portfolios, to make the tracking process more engaging and interactive for both you and your child?

_____

_____

_____

_____

What strategies can you implement to stay organized and manage your homeschooling journey effectively through tracking progress?

_____

_____

_____

_____

How can you make the tracking process a meaningful and fulfilling part of your homeschooling adventure, cherishing the moments of growth and discovery that unfold along the way?

_____

_____

_____

_____

Nine

Homeschooling Hacks and Fun Methods to Make Learning Engaging

Let's embark on an extraordinary expedition to a wondrous realm of creativity and ingenuity! Didn't I make that sound fun? As a homeschooling parent, you recognize that education is not just about pouring information into young minds. It's about incorporating some fun into it as well. The heart of education lies in capturing your child's curiosity, nurturing a lifelong passion for discovery, and hopefully fostering a love for learning. However, we understand that maintaining an engaging and dynamic learning environment can be a challenge, especially when faced with repetitive tasks and seemingly mundane activities. But fear not, for this chapter is dedicated to unveiling a myriad of exciting strategies and practical hacks that will not only infuse exuberance and excitement into your homeschooling routine but also unlock the full potential of your child's educational adventure.

Education is an awe-inspiring journey, a quest for knowledge that should be filled with exploration, wonder, and boundless curiosity. In the realm of homeschooling, you hold the power to orchestrate an extraordinary experience that captures your child's imagination, fuels their thirst for knowledge, and inspires their unique passions. But how can we transform everyday tasks and repetitive drills into captivating escapades? How can we ensure that learning becomes an exhilarating adventure that keeps your children eagerly coming back for more?

In this chapter, we will explore creative homeschooling hacks and fun methods that can transform mundane tasks into enjoyable and educational experiences. By infusing excitement and interactive elements into repetitive tasks, you can keep the momentum going and make learning a fun adventure for your children.

Pairing Fun Activities with Repetitive Tasks

Imagine turning math drills into thrilling treasure hunts, where your child sets off on an adventure to solve equations and unlock secret codes. Or picture transforming vocabulary exercises into captivating word games, where every new word becomes a stepping stone towards building a rich and vibrant lexicon. Note that not every math drill has to be a game, but mixing in some fun with the mundane will offer your children and yourself some relief. With a sprinkle of imagination and a dash of creativity, you can elevate any repetitive task into a captivating challenge that nurtures your child's love for learning.

In the following sections, we will uncover a myriad of inventive ideas and delightful hacks to enliven your homeschooling routine. From captivating science experiments that turn your kitchen into a laboratory of wonders to art projects that transform history lessons into living, breathing masterpieces, you will find an abundance of inspiration to spark your child's enthusiasm for every subject.

So, let's put ourselves into our children's shoes and envision learning from their perspective of what is fun, exciting, and engaging. Let's embark on this thrilling journey of homeschooling hacks and inventive methods that will make learning an exhilarating adventure for you and your children! Let us venture forth, hand in hand, as we unlock the secrets to a world where education and excitement dance harmoniously and every day is a celebration of learning. Together, we can discover the magic that lies within the heart of homeschooling, where curiosity thrives, knowledge flourishes, and the joy of learning knows no bounds.

- Morning Baskets

Imagine starting your homeschooling day with a delightful stack of books, ready to be explored at the breakfast table. Morning baskets are a wonderful way to kickstart the day with engaging and inspiring literature. These baskets can be tailored to include a diverse range of topics, from classic literature and poetry to science books and art appreciation. The key is to choose books that capture your child's interests and curiosity, sparking conversations and discussions that ignite their passion for learning. Encourage your children to share their thoughts and reflections on the stories they encounter.

- Writing Journals

To further enhance the morning basket experience, consider incorporating interactive journals or notebooks, where your children can jot down their favorite quotes, sketch scenes from the stories, or write short book reviews. This not only develops their writing skills but also creates a beautiful keepsake of their educational journey. Encourage all family members to write stories in their individual journals. Set aside time for sharing or even performing these stories, fostering creativity, and strengthening writing skills within a supportive environment.

- Board Games for Phonics

Utilize board games that incorporate phonics exercises to make language arts practice exciting. Children can enhance their reading and spelling skills while having fun with the whole family.

- STEM Exploration

Engage in hands-on STEM activities to explore scientific principles. Conduct science experiments, build models of ecosystems, or explore engineering concepts through fun and interactive projects.

- Mapwork and Geography

Make mapwork interesting by creating maps of your local area. Engage in map-based activities, such as identifying landmarks, planning routes, or conducting virtual tours, to develop map-reading skills and geographical knowledge. Then the opportunity arises also to use these maps for future treasure hunts.

- Create Your Own Quiz Show

Transform history lessons into a lively game by having students create their own quiz show. They can research historical facts, design questions, and host an entertaining quiz competition.

Homeschooling Hacks and Games to Make Life Easier

In the labyrinthine world of homeschooling, navigating the intricacies of day-to-day life can sometimes feel like an odyssey of its own. As dedicated homeschooling parents, you wear many hats—teacher, organizer, cheerleader, and more. Amidst the flurry of lesson plans, assignments, and extracurricular activities, it's only natural to yearn for some ingenious shortcuts and brilliant hacks that make the journey smoother and more enjoyable.

Fear not, for in this section, we delve further into a treasure trove of homeschooling hacks and games designed to streamline your days, lighten your load, and unlock the secrets to a harmonious homeschooling experience. From time-saving tips that free up moments for quality family bonding to organizational marvels that bring a sense of order to your learning environment, these hacks are the magic keys that will make your life as a homeschooling parent a little easier.

We understand the importance of finding balance in your homeschooling adventure, where you can savor precious moments with your children and create lasting memories without being weighed down by the challenges of everyday tasks. So, prepare to unlock a treasure trove of wisdom and ingenuity that will revolutionize your homeschooling routine. Embrace the power of these time-tested hacks, and may they breathe new life into your homeschooling journey, giving every day the possibility of becoming an adventure filled with laughter, learning, and love. Let these homeschooling hacks be more specific, tangible, and helpful examples of ideas to incorporate into your daily and weekly routines.

- Spelling Bee Competition

Organize a spelling bee within your homeschooling environment. This not only helps improve spelling skills but also adds an element of friendly competition, making the learning process engaging and memorable.

- Math Scavenger Hunt

Create a math-themed scavenger hunt where children solve math problems to find hidden clues. This interactive activity enhances problem-solving skills and injects an element of excitement into math practice.

- Reading Challenges

Turn reading time into a game by creating reading challenges. Set goals for the number of books read, explore different genres, or challenge children to find specific themes or elements within the books they read.

- Whiteboard Race

While math is a fundamental subject, it doesn't have to be restricted to traditional worksheets and exercises. Infusing math practice with interactive games can transform it into a fun adventure. Use a whiteboard for math problems and turn solving them into a race. Set up friendly competitions to see who can solve the problem first, adding an element of fun and urgency to math practice.

- Math Games with Minecraft

For children who are drawn to technology and creativity, consider incorporating learning math through Minecraft! Minecraft, a popular digital sandbox game, offers an excellent platform for math exploration. You can create math-related challenges and quests within the game, where your children need to solve math problems to progress in their virtual world. For instance, you can design geometry challenges involving building structures with specific dimensions or multiplication quests that require crafting specific quantities of items.

- Math Games with Cards

If your family enjoys more hands-on activities, traditional card games can be transformed into math adventures. Card games like Uno, Go Fish, or Rummy can be modified to include math facts or number recognition. For example, in Uno, you can assign math operations to each color, and players must answer the math question to play the corresponding card. This playful approach to math practice makes learning enjoyable and memorable.

- History Board Games

Have students create their own board games based on historical events or time periods. This allows them to delve deeper into historical research and gain a comprehensive understanding of the subject matter while enjoying the process.

- Storytelling Challenge

Turn writing into a game by having your children create their own stories. Set prompts or themes and challenge them to develop imaginative narratives, stimulating their creativity and language skills.

- Flashcards for Facts and Concepts

Utilize flashcards to practice facts or concepts in an engaging way. Incorporate visuals, mnemonic devices, or interactive games to make memorization more enjoyable and effective.

- Virtual Field Trips

Take advantage of virtual field trips and turn them into fun learning experiences. Research interactive virtual tours, engage in discussions, and complete related activities to make the most of these educational resources.

- Science Experiment Competition

Organize a science experiment competition where children can showcase their scientific knowledge and creativity. Encourage them to design and conduct experiments, fostering critical thinking and scientific inquiry. Here are a few examples of some popular and engaging science experiments that teach valuable lessons:

- Volcano Eruption: Create a classic baking soda and vinegar volcano to learn about chemical reactions and the release of gases.

- Rainbow Walking Water: Use colored water and paper towels to demonstrate capillary action and how water moves through materials.

- Balloon Rockets: Explore the concept of action and reaction by launching balloon rockets using a straw and string.

- Oobleck: Make a non-Newtonian fluid using cornstarch and water, which behaves like a liquid and a solid depending on the force applied to it.

- Elephant Toothpaste: Witness an exciting chemical reaction that produces a large foamy eruption using hydrogen peroxide, yeast, and dish soap.

- Density Tower: Create colorful layers in a clear container using liquids of different densities, showcasing the principle of density.

- Mentos and Soda Geyser: Drop Mentos candies into a bottle of soda to observe an explosive geyser caused by carbon dioxide bubbles.

- Chromatography Butterflies: Use chromatography paper to separate pigments in markers and create beautiful butterfly designs.

- Egg in a Bottle: Learn about air pressure by using heat to create a vacuum that pulls an egg into a bottle.

- Surface Tension Magic: Experiment with water, soap, and pepper to understand surface tension and how it can be broken.

- Lemon Battery: Generate electricity using lemons and zinc-coated nails to power a small LED light or a clock.

- Solar Oven: Build a simple solar oven using a pizza box and aluminum foil to harness solar energy for cooking.

- Invisible Ink: Use lemon juice or milk as invisible ink and reveal the hidden messages using heat or another chemical.

- Slime: Create different types of slime, such as regular slime, glow-in-the-dark slime, or magnetic slime, to explore polymer properties.

- Static Electricity: Learn about static electricity by rubbing balloons or socks on hair and observing how they attract small objects.

These science experiments offer hands-on experiences that make learning exciting and memorable. They cover various scientific principles, from chemistry and physics to biology and environmental science, fostering curiosity and critical thinking in young minds.

By implementing these homeschooling hacks and fun methods, you can transform repetitive tasks into exciting and engaging experiences to create a vibrant and engaging educational journey for you and your children. Incorporate interactive games, creative projects, and friendly competitions to keep the learning process dynamic and enjoyable for your children. Through the art of pairing fun activities with repetitive tasks, you have learned how to turn seemingly mundane endeavors into opportunities for interactive learning. Your days do not need to be filled with monotony and drudgery; each day has the potential to become a thrilling adventure filled with discovery, wonder, and enthusiasm.

By integrating these homeschooling hacks and fun methods into your daily routine, you can unlock a world of exciting possibilities for your children's learning experience. Embrace the joy of exploring nature while practicing math skills, let your child's imagination soar as they create art while learning history, or embark on a culinary journey that doubles as a science experiment. By infusing you classroom with creativity and engagement, you create an environment where learning transcends the boundaries of textbooks and spills into the realms of excitement and fascination.

Throughout this chapter, we have emphasized the significance of making learning an enjoyable and memorable adventure for your family. Embrace the joy of learning together and cherish the moments of discovery and wonder that unfold each day. As you immerse yourselves in the wonders of homeschooling, I hope you learn to relish the freedom to explore the world at your own pace and to learn not only from textbooks but also from each other.

Remember, the true beauty of homeschooling lies in its flexibility and adaptability. As you embark on this adventure, take the time to observe and understand your children's unique interests and learning styles. With this understanding, you can tailor these hacks and methods to suit their individual preferences, sparking an even deeper passion for learning.

As a homeschooling parent, you have access to a vast array of resources and support networks. Remember to adapt these ideas to suit your children's interests and learning styles, and don't forget to explore reputable educational blogs, online forums, and social media groups to discover more inspiring ideas from like-minded parents and seasoned educators. The homeschooling community is a treasure trove of wisdom and experience, always eager to share innovative approaches that have delighted and inspired their own children.

A few of my personal favorite go-to's for helpful ideas that keep learning and teaching more engaging and enjoyable are.

- **The Homeschool Mom** (www.thehomeschoolmom.com) - This blog offers a wealth of resources, including game ideas, hands-on activities, and creative teaching methods. They provide a variety of free printables and educational games to make learning fun.

- **Homeschool Creations** (www.homeschoolcreations.net) - This blog focuses on homeschooling younger children and provides many printable resources, educational games, and fun learning activities for preschool and elementary-aged kids.

- **Confessions of a Homeschooler** (www.confessionsofahomeschooler.com) - This blog shares practical tips, curriculum reviews, and hands-on learning activities, including games, crafts, and science experiments.

- **Hip Homeschool Moms** (www.hiphomeschoolmoms.com) - This blog offers a supportive community of homeschooling moms and features articles on various topics, including educational games and activities.

- **Wildflowers and Marbles** (www.wildflowersandmarbles.com) - Known for its focus on integrating faith and education, this blog also shares creative ideas for learning games and hands-on activities.

- **The Unlikely Homeschool** (www.theunlikelyhomeschool.com) - This blog provides resources and ideas for homeschooling on a budget, including free educational games and learning hacks.

- **Playdough to Plato** (www.playdoughtoplato.com) - While not exclusively a homeschooling blog, it offers many educational games, activities, and printables that can be used in homeschooling settings.

- **Homeschool Gameschool** (www.homeschoolgameschool.com) - This blog specializes in educational games and board games for homeschooling families, providing reviews and recommendations.

- **Homeschooling with Dyslexia** (www.homeschoolingwithdyslexia.com) - Geared toward families dealing with dyslexia, this blog offers game-based approaches to support learning challenges.

- **Simple Homeschool** (www.simplehomeschool.net) - This blog features a mix of practical advice and creative teaching ideas, including games and fun learning activities.

When exploring these blogs, you'll likely find a wealth of resources, game examples, and teaching hacks that can enhance your homeschooling journey and make learning a joyous adventure for your family.

Embrace the joy of learning together and make homeschooling a memorable adventure for your family. Incorporate interactive games, creative projects, and friendly competitions to keep the learning process dynamic and exciting. Your child's education can be a treasure hunt of knowledge, where every discovery is met with celebration and every challenge becomes an opportunity for growth.

I invite you to hold fast to the magic and spirit of curiosity that infuses homeschooling with boundless potential. Take these homeschooling hacks as your allies and companions on this grand expedition of education. Rejoice in the triumphs, persevere through the challenges, and treasure the shared experiences that knit your family closer together. Homeschooling is not just an alternative to traditional education—it is a lifestyle of lifelong learning, where every moment becomes an opportunity to grow, explore, and thrive as a family united in the love of knowledge.

Now take a moment to review and answer the prompts below. Contemplating these questions allows you to focus on the core ideas presented in the chapter, emphasizing the importance of making learning enjoyable and engaging for children while also highlighting the significance of adapting homeschooling methods to suit individual interests and learning styles. These questions also address the value of utilizing interactive and creative approaches to enhance the learning experience and foster a lifelong love for knowledge in the homeschooling journey and allow you to reflect on which ideas stood out to you as exciting and the best fit for your family.

What were your top 5-10 tips, tricks, or ideas to incorporate some fun into learning?

_____

_____

_____

_____

How can you infuse excitement and interactive elements into repetitive tasks to keep your children engaged and enthusiastic about learning?

_____

_____

_____

_____

What methods do you envision using to teach science and history?

_____

_____

_____

_____

What other creative ideas can you implement to transform math drills and vocabulary exercises into enjoyable and captivating challenges?

_____

_____

_____

_____

What virtual field trips and interactive virtual tours should you incorporate to enhance the learning experience and explore different subjects in an exciting way?

_____

_____

_____

_____

How can you adapt these homeschooling hacks and fun methods to suit your children's unique interests and learning styles to spark a deeper passion for learning?

_____

_____

_____

_____

Conclusion

As we come to the end of this book, it is essential to reflect on the journey we have taken together in the world of homeschooling. This book was never intended to provide all the answers or a one-size-fits-all solution. Instead, it aimed to spark thought, inspire creativity, and offer guidance for those embarking on the homeschooling path. Now, the question remains: Can you see this working for your family?

Throughout our exploration, we have touched upon various key takeaways that can guide you in your homeschooling endeavors. We discussed the importance of understanding your "why" and periodically reassessing whether your approach aligns with your goals. By being kind to yourself and your children, you can navigate the challenges that arise with compassion and create plans that make learning easier and more enjoyable.

Dealing with different age groups together may present its challenges, but it is an opportunity for growth and learning for both you and your children. Finding fun ways to take breaks and infusing joy into your homeschooling routine nurtures a positive environment and strengthens the bond within your family. Putting on an audiobook, playing music for a kitchen dance party, going for a walk outside, or even a quick-timed run around the house can all be excellent ways to break up the day and take a pause whenever you find it's needed.

There will inevitably be days when you feel overwhelmed or "over it." During those moments, remember to take a break, breathe, and engage in activities that uplift your spirit. Separate your children if unhelpful comparisons arise and allow them space when needed, utilizing those moments to complete quick tasks or get some exercise. You'll be getting your steps in as you go back and forth between the two rooms!

Remember that your own self-care is a vital aspect of this homeschooling journey. I encourage you to prioritize your well-being and find ways to rejuvenate yourself, whether it's through a day off, a massage, some sort of physical activity like going for a run or a workout, or simply indulging in a good book. Teaching your children responsibility not only empowers them but also frees up time for other activities. Let them become teachers themselves, encouraging sibling interactions that foster a sense of collaboration and shared knowledge.

As a homeschooling parent, you will embark on a journey of self-discovery, patience, and continuous learning. Make time for personal growth, both intellectually and emotionally, as you guide your children toward becoming their best adult selves. Consider the balance between your work and homeschooling responsibilities, finding ways to integrate or allocate dedicated time for each. Be patient with yourself, especially when you are first starting out. Initially, you will be going back to school yourself, so keep your mind open to learning as well.

Celebrating achievements and milestones, big or small, fosters a sense of accomplishment and motivation within your homeschooling journey. Remember to utilize the resources available to you, such as libraries, beaches, and play parks, to enhance your children's learning experiences. There are so many options you can add to your homeschooling experience.

Lastly, remember that children's comments should not be taken too seriously. Their honesty may sometimes seem harsh, but their perspective is shaped by their immediate experiences. Keep in mind, though, that sometimes they may be right. It's possible that the lesson you're teaching is very boring, so in that instance, choose to engage with your children and brainstorm ways to spice it up! Could they be the teacher? Can you turn it into a game? However, just as important as listening to your children's feedback is, be sure to find someone you can confide in. This should be a trusted individual who can provide support and lend a listening ear during times of frustration and worry. Decompressing alone, with friends, or together as a family helps maintain balance and harmony in your homeschooling routine.

As you progress on this homeschooling journey, always embrace grace. It is a process, a journey of growth and discovery. Homeschooling is not about chasing accolades, badges, or photo-worthy moments. It is about training, teaching, and guiding your children to become their best adult selves. Cherish the journey, for it is a transformative experience that extends far beyond the 12 years of schooling.

May you find joy, fulfillment, and countless meaningful moments as you embark on this homeschooling adventure. With an open heart and a commitment to lifelong learning, you have the power to shape not only your children's futures but also your own. Love the journey, embrace the process, and watch as your family thrives in the realm of homeschooling.

As we conclude this exploration of the homeschooling journey, it is natural to pause and reflect on the insights and guidance that have been shared. From understanding the significance of defining our "why" to embracing the joy of learning together, we have embarked on a transformative experience that extends far beyond traditional education.

Now, as we stand at the crossroads of our homeschooling adventure, it is time to delve deeper within ourselves one last time and ponder the key takeaways from this experience. The questions below will require introspection, guiding you toward a path of purposeful reflection and empowering you to create a vibrant and fulfilling educational experience for yourself and your children. So, with open hearts and inquisitive minds, let us turn our focus inward and explore the last set of questions in closing of our time together. It has been a pleasure to guide you, and I wish you all the best in your homeschooling endeavors! I hope you embark on this wondrous journey with an open heart and a sense of wonder, for the world of homeschooling awaits you with its arms wide open. Happy homeschooling!

After reading this guide in its entirety, has your WHY changed or shifted in any way? Write or rewrite your WHY:

_____

_____

_____

_____

What are your top 3 key takeaways from this guide?

_____

_____

_____

_____

What are your favorite strategies that you plan to implement to make learning easier and more enjoyable?

_____

_____

_____

_____

Does your current approach align with your goals, and do you need to make adjustments to stay on track? If so, what will you adjust?

_____

_____

_____

_____

How can you be kind to yourself and your children during challenging moments in our homeschooling journey?

_____

_____

_____

_____

How will you prioritize your own self-care and find ways to rejuvenate yourself?

_____

_____

_____

_____

How do you plan to handle days when you feel overwhelmed or "over it"?

_____

_____

_____

_____

Appendix: Useful Websites

Chapter 6: Choosing or Creating Your Own Homeschooling Curriculum

- Khan Academy (www.khanacademy.org)

- Time4Learning (www.time4learning.com)

- Oak Meadow (www.oakmeadow.com)

- Calvert Homeschool (www.calverthomeschool.com)

- AmblesideOnline (www.amblesideonline.org)

- Sonlight (www.sonlight.com)

- A Beka Academy (www.abeka.com)

- Homeschool.com (www.homeschool.com)

Chapter 9: Homeschooling Hacks and Fun Methods to Make Learning Engaging

- The Homeschool Mom (www.thehomeschoolmom.com)

- Homeschool Creations (www.homeschoolcreations.net)

- Confessions of a Homeschooler
  (www.confessionsofahomeschooler.com)

- Hip Homeschool Moms (www.hiphomeschoolmoms.com)

- Wildflowers and Marbles (www.wildflowersandmarbles.com)

- The Unlikely Homeschool (www.theunlikelyhomeschool.com)

- Playdough to Plato (www.playdoughtoplato.com)

- Homeschool Gameschool (www.homeschoolgameschool.com)

- Homeschooling with Dyslexia
  (www.homeschoolingwithdyslexia.com)

- Simple Homeschool (www.simplehomeschool.net)

More books by Jane Thome

Homeschooling Planners

Dixie and Dot Children's Books Series

Visit https://jtpublish.com/ to view these books.

About the Author

Scan the code to read more about Jane on Amazon!

Or visit https://jtpublish.com/jane-thome/

Printed in Great Britain
by Amazon

31875245R00069